Astrology and Aptitude:

How to Become What You Are Meant to Be

D1737194

Kim Falconer

ISBN: 0-86690-536-7

First Printing: 2002
Second Edition: 2005

Published by:
American Federation of Astrologers, Inc.
6535 S. Rural Road
Tempe, AZ 85285-2040

Printed in the United States of America

Dedication

This book is dedicated to
D. W. Falconer
My father, astrologer, adventurer,
financial genius and now, spirit guide.

Acknowledgements

I would like to acknowledge the help and support of those special people who have both encouraged and endured my passion for writing and the stars: Eunice F. Mosher, Jan Rae, Jodi Osborne, Lena, (especially Lena), Sue Ellen, young Adam, Dragon, Greg, Iffish, Jamie, Sara and my lovely sister, Sean.

A particular thank you for technical support, staunch enthusiasm and reality checks goes to my brilliant son Aaron Briggs and extreme web master, Tris O'Connor. Heartfelt recognition as well is for Jason Williams, my Oracle and Ly De Angeles, la Strega Magnific.

I warmly acknowledge the wisdom and insights of all my teachers, both here and there, especially D. W. Falconer, John Costa, Lois Gough, Isabel M. Hickey, Joanne Wickenburg, Ivy M. Goldstein-Jacobson, Dennis Elwell, Liz Greene, Howard Sasportas and Richard Idemon.

My deepest gratitude goes to Robert Cooper and the AFA for continual assistance and interest in my work. Appreciation also goes to Eliot Stearnes, Nan Geary, David R. Roell, Zane Stein, Richard Roberts, Jonathan Dunn and Ean Begg for timely direction, enthusiasm, and kind words.

Kim Falconer
June 28, 2001
NSW, Australia

iv

Contents

Introduction

What am I meant to be doing? Is this the right career for me? How can I best develop my skills and abilities? These questions cross the table of many astrologers, guidance counselors and other advisors. They bounce around conversations with friends and over family dinners. They nag quietly in the minds of many who ponder the meaning of life. The search can lead to disillusionment or inspiration. Often it is a mixture of both. Certainly, there can be a deep feeling of inner discontent if we go through life unable to adequately answer the question: *What am I meant to be doing?*

Everyone has proclivities, talents and abilities. It is all a matter of searching them out. We naturally find that some tasks, activities, creative outlets or professions draw our sense of enthusiasm and pleasure much more than others. We also may find that our deeper nature and authentic aptitudes are hidden from sight, leaving an awkward gap. There may be a loss of meaning in life because the instruments of our self-expression are not there, or not being used. We don't live who we really are. The process of finding, mastering and expressing the genuine qualities embedded in each of us is the surest road to self-fulfillment, accomplishment and joy.

Although they bring joy and contentment, innate abilities can be hard to find. Hidden by fear, blocked by doubt and stammered by childhood and social conditioning, sometimes our major talents lie dormant for years. They may even be caught indefinitely in a resistance to *become*: the aversion to *owning* our greatest potential. Conscious or unconscious, these barriers to ability can make us feel frustrated, unworthy and confused about our direction in life. Finding our true and natural aptitudes can mean moving forward once again.

Webster's Dictionary defines aptitude in several ways. It is an innate ability or tendency towards a particular purpose—water seeks its level, oil burns. Aptitude may also be a learned or acquired trait—*she has a fascinating aptitude for the stage.* Aptitude may be a general fitness or suitability as implied in the word *adaptation—they have an aptitude for each other.* Finally, aptitude may describe a basic readiness to lean, achieve or excel in a certain field or endeavor—*the child has a remarkable aptitude.*

In the astrological chart there are specific indications, emphasis in signs, houses or planetary aspects, that point toward our natural talents and abilities. Discovering these indicators in detail and finding ways to enhance, honor and express them can bring a greater sense of well-being, fulfillment and pleasure in life. If we identify and develop our talents and our natural modes of expression, we are free to become everything we can possibly be. This may not always be the panacea to depression, unhappiness, boredom, confusion or the life unfulfilled, yet it is the determinative step in the right direction.

By examining the astrological indicators in the horoscope, we can explore possibilities that will give us the strength and encouragement needed to pursue a life we are meant to be leading. Effort is usually required. Dennis Elwell points this out succinctly in *The Cosmic Loom:* "... *it is a popular delusion that as individuals we automatically grow up into the person we have it in us to be...*"[1]

If we look honestly at the bag of marbles we've been given to play with, how many will we say we used? Which ones did we pick out? Which ones were never touched? Mr. Elwell goes on to suggest: "*Everything the horoscope symbolizes has to be amplified, beefed up! Instead of trying to narrow down its meanings, we have to expand them systematically, explore all the chart's possibilities.*"[2]

This book is a guide to that amplification, that boosting of the chart's indication of our aptitudes, talents, desires and ways of being just who we are. The more we *do* ourselves, the more fulfilled we become, simple as that.

Part I

What's My Line?
Aptitude
and Emphasis by Zodiac

*Whatever you are by nature, keep to it; never
desert your line of talent.
Be what nature intended you for and
you will succeed.—Sydney Smith*

Our basic destiny in terms of talent, aptitude and fulfillment
can be seen in part by the zodiacal position of the planets,
particularly the Sun. Although Sun sign astrology may seem basic
and general, it is the first place to look for meaning and purpose in
the chart.

Like the astronomical body it represents, the Sun in the horoscope shines forth, giving warmth, individuality and distinction to
life. It is the core of the Self, that which we are striving to become. If
we aren't honoring and living out our Sun signs, we aren't being
true to ourselves. Discovering the nature of our natal Sun, and the
other planets as emphasized by sign, can illuminate aptitudes for a
successful and meaningful life. By exploring the zodiac with this
intention, we can learn more about the inner qualities that lead to
fulfillment.

Each zodiacal sign is like a mini culture all its own, with unique
ways and means of getting things done, of sharing and learning and

relating. Each has its own wardrobe, its own desires and its own special orientation toward life. The division of the signs by element, fire, earth, air and water, helps to demonstrate this.

The FIRE signs like to adventure energetically toward new goals. They are vital and naturally full of enthusiasm. The EARTH signs like to build and create in the tangible world. They are grounded and naturally pragmatic. The AIR signs like to communicate rational thoughts and seek knowledge through relationships. They are naturally objective and intellectual. The WATER signs like to feel—pain, pleasure and everything in between. They are sensitive to the things unseen.

For those who have read J.R.R. Tolkein's *The Lord of the Rings*[3], think of the FIRE signs as the riders of the Rohan. Magnificent on their dashing steeds, with shining shields and spears in hand, they pledge to protect the vast plains of their kingdom with energy, enthusiasm and purpose. The race of Hobbits is like EARTH signs with their cozy homes nestled in the side of grassy hills, their love of food and comfort and the building of a good life. Think of the Wizards as AIR signs with their endless study, pursuit of knowledge, spells and divination and their need, sometimes, for solitude as well as communication. Think of the race of Elves as WATER signs, with their deep love for and connection with the environment, their poetry, music, history and stories and their tragic longing for the sundered folk across the distant seas. For those who have not read Tolkein's trilogy, much can be learned about the elements by doing so.

The signs are also divided up into modalities or forms of motion. They are CARDINAL, which is associated with immediate, determined action, FIXED or sustaining, irremovable action and MUTABLE or adaptable, fluid action. Each of the elements has one of its signs in a different modality: Aries is cardinal fire, Leo is fixed fire and Sagittarius is mutable fire. Cancer is cardinal water, Scorpio is fixed water and Pisces is mutable water. Libra is cardinal air, Aquarius is fixed air and Gemini is mutable air. Capricorn is cardinal earth, Taurus is fixed earth and Virgo is mutable earth.

The signs also have a polarity: positive or negative. This is sometimes referred to as Yin and Yang, to avoid dissenting connotations. The positive signs have a tendency toward extroversion, and the negative signs have a tendency towards introversion: Aries is positive or yang and Pisces is negative or yin.

The more we can understand about the nature of the signs that is particularly significant to us, the more we can understand where our aptitude lies. A study of the Sun, Moon and Saturn sign in the individual chart is a good place to start. These are strong points of talent and ability, although not always easy to come by. Any stelliums (a grouping of four or more planets in one sign) can offer a great deal of information as well. Next, every planet's sign needs consideration as a valid indicator of innate talents and abilities in relationship to what that planet represents, as are the angles in the chart (Ascendant, Descendant, Midheaven and IC). Also, note the sign axis of the North and South Lunar Nodes. They can offer extensive insight into life path and direction by their signs, houses and aspects. The key is to look for emphasis that sparks meaning for each individual.

The following delineations of the signs are offered as a guide only. They must be considered with other important areas of the chart and integrated into the whole community of aspects before a complete assessment of aptitude is made. It is also important to remember that everyone has all twelve signs of the zodiac in his or her chart, each taking up residence in a specific area of life, inner or outer, designated by the house cusps. By paying attention to which sign hosts a planet or point or angle in the natal chart, we pay attention to who we authentically are.

Aries as Indicator of Aptitude

Always when warm spring drives winter out and Aries the Ram succeeds to Pisces watery Fish, you rise and blossom on the green turf.[4]

When the Sun, other natal bodies, Ascendant or points fall in the sign of Aries, the warrior wants to emerge. This sign is ruled by the fiery red planet Mars and is symbolized by the lordly Ram. Originally, the representation of the beast showed its head turned back toward its body, an image of self-reflection. Aries is also associated with the Ascendant and the first house of the natural zodiac.

Aries is the first of the FIRE signs and the first of the CARDI-

NAL signs. The operative word is *first*. Aries is a strong indication of aptitude for directness, immediacy, and swift action. Here we have the knight in shining armor, the rescuer, the fighter, the adventurer, a pursuer after the goal unobtainable. The orientation is toward activities that help define the Self, thus the focus on me, myself and I.

Where Pisces wants to merge with the oneness of all life and make no place where one thing ends and another begins, Aries wants to distinguish himself from the crowd, emerging as a separate individual. The results of this intense inner focus can be a capacity for self-direction that makes Aries proficient at being his or her own boss. Not everyone can achieve this—run his or her own business, undertake independent study, grab hold of and control any situation, be the head of the board. Yet for Aries it is a natural state of being.

Aries rules the head and from this word comes many metaphors associated with the sign of the Ram: headstrong, headquarters, making head way, going over someone's head, not to mention, *headache* (for everyone involved) if they can't get their way. These words indicate a sense of leadership and initiative, something Aries has plenty of. Anyone with the Sun or planets in Aries who does not feel in control of his or her life direction will not be a very happy individual. Aries also needs to *get ahead.*

Aptitudes of this sign include taking charge, leadership, control and protection. Aries likes to initiate projects that others can then maintain while they move on to the next challenge. Routine predictable tasks are not for this sign. Aries likes to play, compete and win. He likes to be first. This attribute can have obvious advantages in the fields of athletics, marketing, sales and high finance, national security and medical specialties such as surgery and neurology.

Like the ram, Aries may stamp the earth, drop his head and charge. He can feel at home in occupations that require such skills, including law enforcement—from police officer to attorney—bouncer, bodyguard, martial arts instructor and higher echelons of the military. The important thing for Aries is to have a goal to defend or strive for.

In the film *The Fugitive*[5], Tommy Lee Jones's character, United States Marshall Samuel Gerard, portrays an archetypal Aries figure. He is swift, direct, commanding and bombastic. He has tremendous confidence and focus while the task is at hand and never doubts his course or position.

As with the season of spring, the key talent of Aries is his ability to make things anew. Aries can initiate and work independently of other people. He can also direct others with enormous quantities of energy and enthusiasm, as long as the goal stays fresh. If there is an emphasis in this sign, the individual will not feel fulfilled until these qualities are recognized, cultivated and lived to their maximum capacity.

Taurus as an Indicator of Aptitude

Every man's work, whether it be literature or music or pictures or architecture or anything else, is always a portrait of himself.—Samuel Butler

When the Sun, other planetary placements or angles are in Taurus, the tangible builder emerges. This sign is ruled by the sensual planet Venus, and is represented by the image of the Bull. Whether grazing contentedly in lush fields or charging blindly at fixed objects, this sign contains a measure of tenacity that must not be underestimated. Taurus is also associated with the resourceful second house in the natural chart.

Taurus is the first of the EARTH signs and the first of the FIXED signs. The orientation is toward pleasure and peaceful gratification, away from pain and disruptive upheaval. Taurus has a powerful aptitude for bringing about sustained results, cultivating artistic appreciation and maintaining pragmatic business acumen. There is an innate knack for living the *good life*. Taurus may well be the expert on comfort, repose and delectability. With this sign, sensuality is a must!

Where Aries wants to get things going, assert himself and make a distinct impression of his individuality, Taurus may seem subdued, content to contain energy as opposed to spilling it out in every conceivable direction. Those with this emphasis have an aptitude for sticking with projects, following them through to their ultimate completion. This sign is known for a sustained, if not stubborn, effort.

Taurus rules the neck and throat, and can be known for having a *stiff neck* or even becoming a *pain in the neck,* due to obstinate behavior. The term, *sticking your neck out,* reminds us that risks are not taken lightly with this sign and their awareness of possible results may be more astute than the *come-what-may* attitude of Aries.

Aptitudes associated with Taurus include the ability to garner and develop resources and plan for the future, as in banking, finances, real estate, architecture, building, refurbishing and interior design. Anything that can be seen, touched, tasted and smelled fits the bill, such as gardening, flower arranging, massage, body-work, catering and farming. The artistic nature may flourish through dance, visual and other performing arts, with singing said to be most at home in this sign. They may work with colors, as in fashion, therapy or photography. In the medical field, the focus is on ear, nose and throat or endocrinology. In the alternative medical realm, chiropractic, herbal medicine and homeopathy may appeal.

Taurus wants to respond to a calling that brings practical, tangible results. From politicians to plastic surgeons, from Wall Street brokers to body therapists, this signs needs to get its hands into it and see the actual outcome. Spontaneity is not sought after because this sign prefers a well thought out plan with plenty of comfort stops along the way.

William Hurt plays Dr. Henry Harriston in *A Couch in New York*[6], and this character exhibits some archetypal Taurean behaviors. As a psychoanalyst, his need for order, planning, arranging and containment all represent this sign, as does his culinary talents and sensual awareness. His therapeutic approach is not harsh, his longings for love and intimacy are deeply contained. Thinking of escapes to Paris, his life erupts in turmoil. Simultaneously haunted by circumstances and enchanted by the alluring Beatrice (Juliette Binoche), he eventually finds love and transformation in the end. It is not his words or actions that woo his beloved, but his earthy presence, his tangible being, the sound of his voice, the touch of his fingertips, the integrity of his heart.

Just after the spring of Aries comes the time of gentle nurturing and sustained maintenance that Taurus represents. The sign of the bull keeps things going, steadily and completely. If Taurus can not see his own results, plan for each goal and put ongoing energy into husbanding projects, he will not feel content. With an emphasis in this sign, these are the qualities that must be boosted to feel fulfilled.

Gemini as an Indicator of Aptitude

The only means of strengthening one's intellect is to make up one's mind about nothing—to let the mind be a thoroughfare for all thoughts.—John Keats

When the Sun, Moon, angles or significant planets fall in the sign of Gemini, the reflective thinker emerges. Knowledge becomes power, and communication leads the way. This sign of the twins is ruled by the quicksilver planet Mercury, and *methodical* is not in its bag of tricks. Gemini is associated with the thinking and learning third house of the natural horoscope.

Gemini is the first of the AIR signs and the first of the MUTABLE signs. The orientation is toward concepts, objectivity and exchange of information. The mutable quality makes the sign of the Twins quick-witted, curious and lightening fast to the point of restless. The natural inclination of Gemini is toward communication of all kinds—teaching, learning, reading, writing, speaking, word-processing or just plain talking over a cup of tea. From university lecturers to kindergarten teachers, from authors to counselors, this sign loves to give and receive on a mental level.

Where Taurus is interested in tangible results, Gemini is concerned with thoughts, ideas and themes that reside in the realm of the mind. He can maintain a great effort in any project, as long as it stays interesting and challenging. It must be emphasized that this sign is easily bored. Gemini needs stimulation, not of the body so much as of the intellect.

This third sign of the zodiac is associated with the arms, shoulders and lungs. Gesticulations when they speak, using the hands and arms, are not uncommon. They are certainly a *disarming* sign, although those who know them well are familiar with their ability to keep people at *arm's length*. In association with the lungs, this sign above all others needs plenty of *breathing space*. This propensity allows them to work in fields that require charm and social acumen as well as the ability to work on their own. Those who know

7

the deeper workings of a Gemini also understand their inclination to gain and keep the *upper hand* without ever seeming as if they have done so. Occupations of this nature include journalism, writing, teaching, lecturing, tutoring, counseling and research.

Gemini needs to pursue a calling that can maintain his interest over a sustained period of time. There must be challenge and there must be intrigue. There also must be a sense of communication, whether that consists of an author's readership, an attentive classroom or a client or patient in distress. Gemini's ruling planet, Mercury, was known as the god of commerce and all forms of trade, sales, delivery and exchange are interesting to this sign. Gemini can be very good with languages as well, from computer programming to diplomatic interpretation.

Jeff Goldblume's character in *Independence Day*[7] exhibited some strong Gemini traits. He worked in television broadcasting and communications, was quick witted and thought fast on his feet. He came up with solutions from his position of objectivity, zipped around the city on a bicycle and played a mean game of chess. His dialog, internal or external, never seemed to stop. We certainly never saw him sitting still. In this case, it was his ideas, generated through conceptualization and expressed by clear and convincing articulation, that saved the day.

After the rush of spring growth and the establishment of life come the early summer of Gemini with its longing for reason and desire to communicate. If those with planets in this sign are not fulfilling these desires—if Gemini is unable to ponder ideas, seek knowledge and gather facts to later express and converse about—they will not feel complete, fulfilled or successful.

Cancer as and Indicator of Aptitude

And it's Oh! In my heart, I wish him safe at home.—Dorthea Jordon

When the Sun, Moon, Ascendant or significant planetary placements fall in the sign of Cancer, a longing for safety, protection and nurturing emerges. This is the sign of the archetypal MOTHER and how can that image be complete without an offspring to nurture? Cancer, imaged by the silent sea crab, is ruled by the ever-changing

Moon and associated with the fourth house of the natural horoscope.

This is the first of the WATER signs and the second of the CARDINAL signs. The orientation is toward feeling, intuition and initiation through the emotions. The cardinal quality makes the sign of the crab powerful and stalwart in its ability to grab a belief, drive or project and hold on until the mission is accomplished. The natural inclination of Cancer is toward the sharing of genuine feelings from joy to sorrow, from agony to ecstasy. This is one of the few signs that is not afraid of pain. From musicians to chefs, scientists to mountain climbers, Cancer's strength lies in the ability to plumb the feeling depths of the soul.

Where Gemini is concerned with the landscapes of the mind, Cancer is drawn to the world of the feelings. There is tremendous intuition here, with a strong measure of caution. Cancer will not want to venture forth until there is an assurance of security. Cancer likes things to be safe, they may not express much until a measure of invulnerability or protection is felt. They cannot be pushed easily in this respect or in any respect.

Cancer rules the breast or mammary glands, giving us every child's name for the primary care-giver: *Mammy, momma, mom, mummy, mum, ma.* There is no dispute about Cancer's association with mother. The sign of the crab also rules the stomach that extracts nourishment for the rest of the body, and this is the sign noted for its natural *gut feelings.* There may not be a rational explanation why a decision has been reached: They go for it because it *feels right in their gut,* or it is declined because *they didn't have the stomach for it.* Either way, when Cancer people are finished mulling things over, they usually make the right choice for them. Being a WATER sign, these choices are made mostly by non-rational means.

Like the other WATER signs, Cancer needs to feel connected and has a strong sense of relationship to the environment. What seems like a natural sense of space to the air or fire signs can feel like abandonment or rejection to Cancer. They want to be close, connected and secure, and their aptitudes lie in the realm of sensitivity to others, individually or collectively, and to the world around them.

This opens up all forms of creativity—music, poetry, visual arts, performing arts and dance—in ways that reach deep into the heart and express not so much ideas but feelings. Any field of endeavor may be approached with great nurturing and sensitivity, be it the healing arts, from neurosurgeon to midwife, homeopath to chiropractor, environmental science to teaching or tutoring. The helping professions, childcare and any talent that surrounds and protects—security, catering, counseling, gardening—may be areas of life that blossom for those born with planets in Cancer. They also may be attracted to writing, politics, history, things of the past, and business of all kinds. Cancer has a special relationship with money. They like it, need it and don't want to let it go.

Money for Cancer may be more a symbol for security than it is for the other signs. Taurus may see money as power, Gemini may find it a means of exchanging ideas, Aries may approach it as a factor to the next adventure, but for Cancer, money can be seen a lifeblood. It is best not to stand between a Cancer and his or her funds.

Holly Hunter's role as Ada in *The Piano* portrays some archetypal characteristics of Cancer. She is a single mother of a female child, both *abandoned* to an unknown life in the costal wilderness of New Zealand. Ada is a strong woman, creative, passionate and also mute. Expressing herself through music, her silence does not hinder her power. Neither does it protect her from emotional pain, mutilation and betrayal. The haunting beauty of this character expresses in soundlessness what could never be said in words.

Cancer shines in the summer of nourishment and steady growth through loving, caring and sometime culling hands. Without the opportunity to give and receive creative nurturing to themselves and others in this way, Cancer will not feel fulfilled.

Leo as an Indicator of Aptitude

Put yourself on view. This brings your talents to light.—Baltasar Gracian

Those born with the Sun, Moon or significant planets or points in Leo best allow the sovereign lion to awaken. Ruled by the life giving Sun, this is the sign of the monarch, the actor, the master of all he beholds. The second of the FIRE signs and the second of the

FIXED signs, Leo the lion, king of the beasts, has great stores of energy along with the ability to sustain whatever is initiated. This sign is associated with the expressive and romantic fifth house of the natural horoscope.

The innate orientation of Leo is toward creativity, performance, allegiance, command and generosity. They have a flare for drama because, as with all the fire signs, they like to mythologize life. The ordinary is shunned in favor of a grander scale of existence (in heart and deed, if not in practicality).

They prefer to travel first class, arrive with a bang and leave a crowd breathlessly applauding. This holds just as true for business meetings and first dates as it does for dental appointments and job interviews. A command performance is what counts. There is nothing commonplace about Leo, and it is best not to attempt too prosaic an existence with planets or points in this sign.

The aptitudes of the lion may shine in any project that requires leadership, courage and creativity. This sign revels in the light of attention and these people will give one hundred percent of themselves when their heart is engaged. They have a youthful approach to life that brings with it stimulation, optimism and enthusiastic zeal. These are qualities that need to be encouraged in any Leo, no matter what age.

Unlike Cancer, who is concerned with the deep and sometimes murky realm of feelings, Leo is interested in the light of creative self-expression. This creativity is usually playful and interactive, needing someone to share it with. Like all the FIRE signs, they will dramatize events to ensure attention and participation. They are not often afraid of creating a *scene*.

Leo is associated physiologically with the heart, and words like *lion heart, warm hearted and kind-hearted* all relate. If someone is particularly generous—a Leo trait—we say they are *big hearted*. If they no longer feel love or creative inspiration, we say they have *lost heart*. Leo thus symbolizes those things that awaken or engage the heart, such as romance, theater, music, drama, the arts and creations of all kinds, including children. Leo is also associated with courage, a word derived from the middle French word *cuer* or *heart!*

Whatever Leo does, the talent lies in the delivery. This sign needs to make an impact, be it in the financial world, the arts, medicine, music, literature, helping professions, education or more primary fields such as produce, animal husbandry and businesses of all kinds. Technical skills such as laboratory work, information technology, wood and metal craft may also arise as talents, executed with typical Leo style. The main prerequisite is the unlimited nature of the field and the ability to enjoy the freedom and power of self-direction. Leo wants to gain as much domain as possible and really needs to be his or her own boss, although many will not appreciate working in isolation. The need for camaraderie, and/or an audience, is ever present.

Sean Connory's renowned characterization of agent 007 in the film *Goldfinger*[8] portrays the charismatic, mysterious and incredibly sophisticated individual that meshes with the Leo archetype. As James Bond, he wields the power that instills fear in his enemies and gains respect from his peers and irresistible sexual attraction from friend or foe. His actions are dramatic, precise and usually come just in the nick of time. Everything he touches turns to excitement, with him right in the thick of it.

Leo is born in the drama of mid-summer, where flowers bloom, fruits ripen and leaves shimmer in the light of the long days. This sign has the sustaining and brilliant ability to bring life's projects to the stage and well laid plans to fruition.

Any Leo who is unable to shine, to garner respect and admiration in a trade or profession, to be appreciated for special abilities and to climb to the heights of individual potential will feel unfulfilled. He must have respect, beginning with respect for himself. Any Leo who is sequestered in a common life with no room for creative uniqueness will be a wretched Lion, one without hope or glimmer.

Virgo as an Indicator of Aptitude

If I have ever made any valuable discoveries, it has been owing more to patient attention, than to any other talent.—Isaac Newton

Those born with the Sun, Moon or significant planets or points in the sign of Virgo had best be prepared to let the investigator in. The Sherlock Holmes of the zodiac, Virgo's talents lie in an astute at-

12

tention to detail, a relentless sense of pursuit and the ability to bring order to any puzzle presented. Ruled by the quick wit of Mercury, Virgo is the second of the EARTH signs and the second of the MU-TABLE signs, symbolized by the divine virgin/harlot. This combination unites pragmatic sensibilities with a fluid and flexible approach. Virgo, who also links with the industrious sixth house of the natural horoscope, has them both.

Any task, profession, art or trade that requires the skillful and detailed, discerning and critical approach will suit Virgo just fine. They tend to be critical sometimes, although that is mainly due to the innate perceptions that compare and contrast with such lucid ease and necessity. This sign brings order to chaos, whether it is asked for or not.

Where Leo wants to rule, command and perform, Virgo is much more content to be the power behind the throne. Not needing or seeking the public recognition of the Lion, Virgo wants to produce for the innate satisfaction that the process brings. Like all the EARTH signs, they prefer to see a tangible result and, unique to themselves, they may not reveal those results until they deem them accomplished. This is a sign that likes to practice and perfect in private, working sometimes in isolation for long periods of time before the *product* of that work is revealed. They will only show off a finished result when they deem it worthy.

Virgo relates to the small intestines and the spleen. Both these organs share a function of assimilation/filtration where, in the former, nutrients are distinguished, categorized and absorbed and, in the latter, bacteria and particulate matter, such as worn out red cells, are selectively removed from circulation. The metaphor here is one of minute and differential categorizing, a Virgo strong point. The word *intestine* means *internal* and symbolizes much of Virgo's propensity for introspection and inward looking nature. Sometimes Virgos are also known for their critical irritability, as portrayed by the middle English and old French association of the spleen with ill-humor, peevish or irritable attitudes, as in the word *spleenful.*

For Virgo, happiness and fulfillment lie in the details of craft or profession. This can range from accounting, dentistry, vascular surgery and computer systems analysis to animation, make-up artistry, nursing and education fields of all kinds. The emphasis is on taking everything down to its component parts, be it an automobile, a living-organism, an architectural design or a statistical analysis. *Virgo wants to get to the finer details, and any task, art, craft or profession that allows for that will be rewarding.*

Mia Farrow's character in Alice[9] portrays the Virgo archetype with her analytical wit, concern with propriety, the fluctuation between insecurity and paranoia to absolute confidence, the complexity of inter-relationships and the constant stream of mercurial thought. She seeks the help of a Dr. Yang's magic herbs and eastern philosophies help her out of her meaningless routine and into a more authentic self. She experiences the shadow Pisces longing for her lost youth love while also fantasizing about a new lover who happens to be a musician. Through transformation and separation from all her previous supports and identities, her character remain heroic, eventually finding independence and meaning in her own right.

Virgos are born at the beginning of the harvest season when fruits and crops and herds must be evaluated for readiness. It is a time of hope of plenty. A time of concern for the garnering of the future.

If Virgo cannot deal in the capacity of fine details, if they can not use their expertise to distinguish between minute component parts, if they can not see the tangible results of their efforts, they will not feel fulfilled. Virgo must use their critiquing efforts to the maximum, bringing organization to anarchy.

Libra as an Indicator of Aptitude

For beauty being the best we know
Sums up the unsearchable and secrete aims
Of nature.—Robert Bridges

Those born with the Sun, Moon, Ascendant or other planets and points in the sign of Libra need to awaken the lover of beauty, balance and veracity. They seek truth in the context of rational thought and live to recreate the world in accordance to their observations and beliefs. This may be a very beautiful world.

Ruled by Venus, goddess of love, Libra is the second of the AIR signs and the third of the CARDINAL signs. This combination

14

brings out an innate ability to initiate through objective reasoning, communication, and sense of what is fair and just, as represented in their symbol, the inanimate Scales. Libra also links to the partnering seventh house of the natural horoscope.

This is the sign of the skilled statesman, the diplomat, the keeper of the peace though fairness, facilitation and if necessary, distraction. Libra above all wants to make everything nice, with everyone mingling happily and all their wishes fulfilled. That is, unless things go wrong. At that point, Libra can become the devil's own and well-versed advocate, creating debate and animated discussions where once only daisies grew. Remember, the goal is balance.

Where Virgo wants to bring order to chaos, Libra wants to bring opposites into harmony. This may be accomplished by means of tact and artful diplomacy or, if that fails, by means of intellectual disputation. Like all AIR signs, Libra functions from the intellect, the realm of rational thought, and what really matters to them, above the tangible, are the words. To them, what one says is often more important than what one actually does.

Libra relates physically to the kidneys and adrenal glands. The adrenals produce the steroid adrenaline, closely linked to balancing the immune system and vital for fight or flight. The kidneys function to maintain fluid balance in the body, regulate acid/base balance and excrete metabolic waste. The operant theme here is *balance.* Like the archetype of Libra, the kidneys and adrenals function to maintain equilibrium within a closed system. The word *kidney* used to refer to ones disposition and was associated with temperament. This links to the word *temper,* to modify, to moderate, to mix suitably, to follow the middle course on either side of two extremes. We all know what can happen if we *lose our temper.*

For Libra, fulfillment lies in the creation of balance, beauty and the goodness of truth. Occupations that reflect this need include fine arts, music, beauty therapy (from plastic surgery to cosmetics), clothing design and importation, diplomacy and law, florists and jewelers, counselors and therapists, architects and town planners. Anything that allows Libra to feel it is contributing to the improvement of their environment, large or small, is potentially rewarding. Doctors, veterinarians, environmentalists, musicians and publishers all might fit the bill. One thing to remember about Libra is these people seldom like to get their hands dirty and prefer to work in as pleasant and aesthetically pleasing surroundings as possible.

Keanu Reeves' character in *The Devils Advocate*[10] portrays some elements of the archetype of Libra. As Kevin Lomax, he is a sharp, intelligent lawyer, upwardly mobile, concerned with image, the law and his own ambition. He wants the glamour of a beautiful home and successful career. He is enchanted, for a time, with the things his money can buy. He tries to keep everyone happy, devil or saint, and justifies all his actions, one way or another, until he sees the truth behind the deceptions. At that point, he takes drastic measures to stand corrected, to rectify his error in judgment and perception. Paradoxically, that means he starts all over again, with yet another series of choices.

Libras are born in the fullness of the harvest season where fruits and crops and herds are at their peak. It is a time for feasting, celebration and relating, a time of communication and socializing. If Libra cannot join in, share ideas, form relationships and create a balance for the future, he or she will not feel fulfilled. Libra must use its eye for beauty, equilibrium and refinement in every way it can.

Scorpio as an Indicator of Aptitude

Everyone has talent. What is rare is the courage to follow the talent to the dark place where it leads.—Erica Jong

Those born with the Sun, Moon or significant planets and points in the sign of Scorpio need to walk on the edge of life, awakening the depths of their souls through risk and intensity. Scorpion or Phoenix, they must develop a sense of trust that can only come through leaping into the darkness of the unknown, a place of no guarantees.

Ruled by Pluto and Mars, gods of death and war respectively, Scorpio is the second of the WATER signs and the third of the FIXED signs. This combination brings out an innate ability to merge energy with others and create a lasting transformation. Scorpio also links to the mysterious eighth house of the natural horoscope.

16

This is the sign of sex, death and change, the inevitable components of life. An emphasis in this sign can express in myriad ways, from doctors, especially emergency room and surgical specialists, health professionals, crisis counselors, ambulance drivers and therapists to secret agents, tax collectors, undertakers, sex workers and snake handlers. Scorpio above all wants to have intensity with others, and is willing to risk a great deal to achieve that goal. They can express themselves with great passion, through speaking, acting, writing, painting, dancing, and performing arts of all kinds. They don't do it for the glory of it all, like Leo; they do it to take risks, to express and commune with power, to feel alive.

Where Libra wants to bring opposites into balance, Scorpio wants to merge energy with passion to create a kind of lasting alteration. They may do this with subtle control or wholesale destruction. It is not always easy to predict which. Like all WATER signs, Scorpio functions through the realm of feelings and is not afraid of emotional pain. Any occupation that allows them to use this attribute will enhance their feelings of well-being.

Scorpio relates physiologically to the regenerative organs of both sexes, symbolizing the power of creation within each one of us. The word *genitals* comes from the Latin root *genitalia*, a derivative of the early Greek *gene,* or *born.* Many words relate to Scorpio through this link: Something that produces or is produced as in *oxygen or antigen,* the functional hereditary unit, *gene,* to bring into existence, *generate* or *generator,* to share or give with willingness, *generosity* or *generous,* one who creates, *genitor,* and finally, one of exceptional intellect or creative power, a *genius,* is one who's prevailing spirit or god presides over their birth and life. The depths that Scorpio seeks are no less profound than the anatomy associated with this sign.

For Scorpio, fulfillment lies in the depths though the exploration of mysteries, research, or practical communication with others in ways that are not ordinary or mundane. Occupations that reflect this need include anything that allows Scorpio to feel the balance of life and death. They are known to put their life on the line, over and over again. From research scientists handling dangerous microbiotics to characters in Macbeth, from volunteer rescue teams to test pilots and skydivers, this sign needs to visit the edge. They will never feel fulfilled unless they do so on a fairly regular basis.

Jack Nicholson's characterization of publisher Will Randall in the film *Wolf*[11] portrays the archetype of Scorpio and not just because the power of the wolf is central to the theme, although that counts. In this story, Mr. Randall has a mystical encounter with the animal side of his nature and finds he is regaining his eroded sense of power and authority. He proceeds to live out more and more of his potential as the wolf in him grows. As an associate editor of a major publishing company and about to be retrenched, he takes an enormous gamble and succeeds. His intimate relationships become intense to the extreme and his drive and vitality deepen with every risk. In the end, it is a struggle to the death with his dark side, a twisted and manipulative foe. The interesting thing is, like Scorpio, the power of the wolf is impartial, neither particularly good or particularly evil. It is distinctly up to the individual's discretion how the energy is used.

Scorpios are born at the end of the harvest when survival is based on the results of the past. In North America, it is the time of Thanksgiving, a time of sharing the summer's productive bounty with others and of turning thoughts inward with the darkening days. If Scorpio is unable to regenerate, to share and merge with others in profound ways and delve into the mysteries that lie under the surface, he will not be accomplished. Scorpio must feel that whatever he does, from catering a wedding to lecturing in front of rocket scientists, is a mater of life and death.

Sagittarius as an Indicator of Aptitude

Better to light a candle than to curse the darkness.—Chinese Proverb

Those born with the Sun, Moon or significant planets or points in the sign of Sagittarius need to feel the freshness of new opportunities, the exuberance of enthusiasm and the unlimited freedom of endless possibilities. Ruled by Jupiter, king of the Olympians, Sagittarius is the third of the FIRE signs and the third of the MUTABLE signs. This goes a long way to describe the Archer's abundant eagerness to embrace life, his love of new and extensive horizons and the burning desire to explore the unknown. Sagittarius also links to the philosophical ninth house of the natural horoscope. In this sign, explorations are based on a search for truth and meaning. Whatever Sagittarius does, it wants the feeling that goals and opportunities are boundless. A trapped, cornered or restricted Archer is not a happy sight. It is certainly not a fulfilled individual.

An emphasis in Sagittarius can express in a range of occupations, including aviation, philosophy, religion, law, education—especially university levels—and all jobs that allow for communication of beliefs and travel. This travel can be tangible, as in production companies, airline personnel, and art dealers, or more philosophical, as in scientists, philosophers or teachers and writers of all kinds. It can have a sense of the mystical, as in those on a spiritual quest or even in more orthodox religious positions. Sagittarius people can also be very playful and buoyant, making them excel in theater, acting, directing, politics and public speaking.

Where Scorpio wants to merge energy with passion to create a kind of lasting alteration, Sagittarius seeks to discover and communicate the truth, meaning and purpose of life. Like all FIRE signs, they do this with energy, enthusiasm and a rich gusto that the rest of us find hard to resist. Any occupation that allows them to use these attributes will enhance their feelings of well-being. Sagittarius relates to the hips and thighs, and it is interesting that the Archer's penchant for keeping up with currents trends in some circles is known as being *hip*. Sagittarius also relates to the gall bladder and this sign is known at times for an innate imprudence: *he had the gall to tell me I was wrong.* It is also associated with the liver, once thought to be the main producer of life giving blood. The word *liver* comes from the root word *leip* and relates to *life, living* and the act of being *lively*. One of the most obvious traits of a Sagittarius is their energetic, optimistic and life affirming disposition.

For Sagittarius, fulfillment lies in the canopy of endless possibilities. Anything that says *the sky's the limit* will intrigue them, anything that requires a lot of communication—from phone time to one-to-one or group discussions—will keep them interested. Getting stuck in mundane routine or boring, predictable exercises will dull their interest, turning them away to seek new possibilities. Sagittarius needs fresh goals and new challenges. Like all the MUTABLE signs, they can get bored extremely quickly.

Harrison Ford's character, Indiana Jones, in *Raiders of the Lost Ark*[12] portrays many aspects of the archetypal Sagittarius. He is a professor of archeology and lecturer at university and also a daring explorer—an adventurous man who travels the world in search of a rare and mystical artifact. He faces enemies with a sense of optimism and humor, never giving up faith in the possibility of success and survival. He is a hero in the fiery, majestic, self-assured and charismatic tradition with the added benefit of a tertiary education.

Sagittarians are born at the darkest time of year, when the days reach their shortest hours and are yet to build slowly towards the promise of a future summer. Long nights may be spent philosophizing, sharing experiences and indulging in the stores of the harvest, food and wine alike. If Sagittarius is unable to communicate, strive towards the unknown and seek after truth with the gift of enthusiasm, he will not feel a sense of joy and fulfillment in life.

Capricorn as an Indicator of Aptitude

I know of no more encouraging fact than the unquestioned ability of a man to elevate his life by conscious endeavor.—Henry David Thoreau

Those born with the Sun, Moon or significant planets or points in the sign of Capricorn need to embrace their healthy ambition, overcome fears of failure and strive to build a world that merges tangible reality with the mystical occult. Living out the symbol of the Sea-goat, half mammal and half cold blooded serpent, is not an easy task.

Ruled by Saturn, usurped king of the Titans, Capricorn is the third of the EARTH sign and the fourth of the CARDINAL sign of the zodiac. This helps explain the Sea-goat's powers of initiation, ambition and aspiration. Capricorn also links to the career oriented tenth house of the natural horoscope.

This sign is the builder of earthly dreams and ambitions, the cool and contained individual, the calculating and the aloof. This is also the sign of the mystic who delves into the inner exploration of self, the unconscious, and all things ancient and occult. Sometimes Capricorn is one or the other—mystic or pragmatist—but to be truly happy, he needs to work in both worlds. He also doesn't mind struggling to reach a goal or maintain existence, whether admitted or not.

An emphasis in Capricorn can express in a range of occupations including fields of business and management, finance, science, chemistry, mathematics and medicine (especially orthopedics, dentistry and dermatology). They may become carpenters, brick layers, chiropractors, civil engineers or clock makers, or involve themselves in the helping professions, (particularly those dealing with depression), quarry workers, gardeners, government officials or politicians. Capricorns can be teachers of all kinds, from kindergarten to university levels. It is their traditional and thorough style of teaching (task-master) that distinguishes them. They appreciate the past and may work with *old* things: antiques, wine, art, or restorations, even geriatrics.

Where Sagittarius seeks to discover and communicate the truth, meaning and purpose of life, Capricorn seeks to build a tangible representation of their ability to survive and master in the world at large (real or occult). They want, above all, to be self-sufficient. They abhor dependency and neediness of all kinds and like all EARTH signs, they have a tactile approach that uses what can be seen, touched, tasted and felt to express themselves. In the arts—dance, music, visual, film—they express less in words than in the optical.

Capricorn is associated physically with all structures that give support including bones and joints in the body, teeth and the protective skin. Where Capricorn is by sign in the natal chart is where we need *backbone,* where we need strength and courage to stand up and face all that may come. If life's tasks become too arduous, we say that they are *back-breaking* or we do not have the *spine* for it. If we have no willpower left, we are *spineless* (boneless invertebrates). If we are oversensitive to criticism, we are said to be *thin-skinned.* If we can take injustice or verbal abuse with composure, we are said to be *thick-skinned.* If we have *a bone to pick* there is a dispute to straighten out. If we *make no bones about it,* we are going to be completely candid and if we *feel it in our bones,* we are feeling the roots of our intuitive powers. These metaphors all point to the issues of strength, patience, judgment and capability that Capricorn represents symbolically through his skin and bones.

Fulfillment lies in the ability to achieve accredited recognition. They want the rubber stamp. They want the degree, the certification and the acknowledgment that comes with accredited public approval. If given a choice between a certificate or degree program of study and work experience, Capricorn would be wise to take the certification path. Capricorn also needs to prepare for a future that is self-maintaining. They want to know they can survive on their own, regardless of how many others are willing to support them or cooperate.

Capricorn, like Sagittarius, needs fresh goals and new challenges, not so much because they get bored easily, but because they must prove themselves, again and again. As with all CARDINAL signs, Capricorn needs to initiate and deal with issues of leadership, power and control. Any occupation that helps them do this, will lead to a greater sense of self.

Peter O'Toole's character in *Lawrence of Arabia*[13] portrays many aspects of the archetypal Capricorn. He is a man born illegitimately and does not know his father. Thus begins his search for self with no map or model to steer by (though his job as a lieutenant in the British Army has him coloring in maps). He is a loner and goes willingly into the desert on a quest no one suspects he will achieve. He struggles to unite a people who first have no concept that they even are a people. As he struggles to unite the Bedouins to fight against the Turkish forces, often at the disapproval of those in authority over him, he finds parts of himself. With goals that are based on a complex mix of personal glory and humanitarian cause, this conflicted man builds himself a reputation larger than life. It is his striving for success that brings him deeper and deeper into the well-spring of his own spirituality.

Capricorns are born at the winter solstice, a time of festivity. Traditionally, the renewal king is born at this time, bringing hope and promise for a longed-for future. The king appears at the darkest time of year, when the days reach their shortest hours and build slowly toward the future summer. This is a time of celebration and, for many, an arduous preparation for expected meals, company and the giving of tangible gifts. It may also be a time of spirituality, renewal of love and acceptance. Capricorn, to be fulfilled, must embrace all these symbolic aspects of their auspicious birth.

Aquarius as an Indicator of Aptitude

I have heard something very shocking indeed . . .—Jane Austen

Those born with the Sun, Moon or significant planets in the sign of Aquarius need to appreciate the great awakener inside them. They thrive by embracing the freedom loving, idealistic, off-beat and forward thinking qualities this archetype represents. Aquarius' symbol, the Water-bearer, pours forth the knowledge, feelings and ideals of human nature without ever getting his own hands wet. This shows how Aquarius may be at times aloof in a social sense. He is more at home with the idea of camaraderie than actually hanging out with friends, yet still Aquarius disseminates wisdom and is an inflamer of ideals with genuine conviction and concern.

Ruled traditionally by Saturn, the King of the Titans, and in the last century co-ruled by Uranus, god of the starry skies, Aquarius is the third of the AIR signs and the fourth of the FIXED signs. This describes the Aquarian ability to grab an idea and hold on tight. Aquarius also links to the goal and group oriented eleventh house of the natural horoscope.

This is the sign of the objective thinker, the idealist, the revolutionary, the one not afraid of the future. They observe life from afar and have sometimes established ideas on how things should or could be changed, or might be better. Part of their aptitude lies in this ability to objectify life, to detach and separate content from context.

An emphasis in this sign can express in a range of occupations, including aeronautic engineer, scientist (especially research), communicator (radio and TV announcers), astrologer, inventor, politician, color therapist, counselor and anything new age and/or electrical: electrician, computer operator, 3D animator, system analyst, programmer, television and radio personnel, lighting or sound engineer, therapist, social worker and telephone operator. Anything that connects, communicates, disseminates and reforms is a healthy Aquarius occupation.

Where Capricorn seeks to build a tangible representation of its ability to survive and master in the world at large (real or occult), Aquarius seeks to communicate ideas and make radical changes where outlived values are being served. They want, above all, to bestowed a sense of freedom on humankind, taking the fire of the intellect and creative force from the hands of the gods and placing it into the hands of the human race.

Like all AIR signs, they have a strong need for space, freedom and, above all, to honor the communication of words in the written of spoken form. They may excel in any creative venture as long as they have a sense of self-authority and are able to articulate their idealized vision. They could have some difficulty taking direction from others if they do not respect or hold in high regard the director. Because of this, they often work best at the top or on their own.

Aquarius is associated physically with the ankles, which allow us to walk forward and upright, and the cardiovascular circulatory system. For something to *circulate*, it must have freedom of movement or passage through its given system and the ability to gather along the way and then return to its source. Aquarius lives this out with their need to *circulate*, to flow freely with their ideas in groups, with friends and in associations. If someone's ideas are in vogue, we say they are in *circulation* because they are being passed about, are widely known or in the process of being *picked up*. Aquarius is also associated with the blood, and words like *blood-brothers*, and *kindred blood*, all fit in with the Aquarius ideal to unite in the brotherhood of humankind.

For Aquarius, fulfillment lies in the ability to achieve a sense of circulated ideas, organization and delegation of power, and a sense that what they are doing has specific relevance to the advancement of the group. They can get bored easily and need to work with a variety of challenges to hold their interest. Aquarius needs unique goals to feel alive, even if they are of a surprising, shocking or upsetting nature. They also need to feel they can assert their will and maintain a sense of freedom and autonomy in any given situation. As with all FIXED signs, Aquarius will hang on to a project to mold and develop it. Occupations that help them do these things with a flare of originality will lead to a greater sense of self.

Julia Roberts's Oscar winning role as *Erin Brocovich*[14] portrays this Aquarian sense fighting for the rights of the public with great tenacity and will. A single mother, Erin adamantly claims the right to a job to support her three children and her own right to develop herself through the pursuit of a social injustice: contaminated drinking water. She shocks, pushes, demands and cajoles her way to success, fighting for the underling that has no power or voice. Her victory becomes the victory of the masses as she brings a corporate giant to its knees, exposing their negligence. Not by traditional education, connections or know-how, but by sheer will does she triumph.

Aquarians are born before the spring, when the thought of life reawakening is only a vision. It is a time to contemplate, plan and discuss, a time to research and think towards the future. For Aquarius to be happy, he must find ways to express ideas to the fullest benefit of humankind, aiming to be everything he can possibly become.

Pisces as an Indicator of Aptitude

When we were children, we used to think that when we were grown-up we would no longer be vulnerable. But to grow up is to accept vulnerability. . . . To be alive is to be vulnerable.—Madeleine L'Engle

Those born with the Sun, Moon or significant planets or points in the sign of Pisces need to appreciate the poetic dreamer in the depths of their soul. They thrive by acknowledging their own mysteries side by side with more tangible aspects of life. Pisces may be a mathematician or a metallurgical engineer, but also must quench a thirst for spirit that can not be ignored without consequence. Those who do ignore the spirit may take other paths—the well-known propensity of this sign for drugs, alcohol and other abusive forms of escape. The Pisces symbol, Two Fishes swimming in opposite directions yet tied together exemplify this dichotomy—power in the real world, power in the spiritual world. Pisces must look to both.

Ruled traditionally by Jupiter, King of the Olympians, and more recently by Neptune, the King of the underwater realm, Pisces is the third of the WATER signs and the fourth of the MUTABLE signs. This describes Pisces ability to move in and out of boundaries as if they were very thin veils. The intuition is strong, the emotions accessible, the psychic ability pronounced. Pisces also links to the mysterious twelfth house of the natural horoscope.

This is the sign of the sensitive creator, the visionary, the explorer of the hidden world of feelings. Part of their aptitude lies in the ability to reach down into the sea of the collective unconscious and bring up something new and relevant for the rest of humankind. They may paint it, dance it or play it as a symphony. They may write it down in a book or express it as an equation on a blackboard. However they do it, the rest of the world usually sighs, *ah*.

An emphasis in this sign can express in a range of occupations, including actor, chemist, fashion designer (especially foot wear), health professional (especially working in hospitals and in anesthetics), lifeguard, private investigator, occultist, religious professional, rescue worker, retreat/health/rehab operator, swimmer, diver, offshore oil dweller, marine biologist, fisher, physicist, writer, poet and poison control manager. Anything that allows Pisces individuals to dip into that other realm, be it spiritual studies, psychology, arts, dance, drama or mathematics, will help them to feel fulfilled.

Where Aquarius seeks to communicate ideas and make radical changes where outlived values are being served, Pisces wants to merge with the oneness of all life and make no place where one thing ends and another begins. They want to feel deeply connected to something or someone they believe in. They want to appease their divine homesickness though a life long search for the ineffable.

Like all WATER signs, they have a strong need for emotional rapport, be it through love relationships, family, creativity or discovery. They do not want to feel alone, although many do spend time in isolation of some sort. Their sense of connection is so profound, it usually brings disappointment to many experiences. Reality can rarely match the acuteness of their imagination.

Pisces is associated physically with the feet, the part of the body that relates to faith and understanding. When we are overcome with emotion, we are *knocked off our feet* and when we are filled with romantic love we are said to be *swept off our feet*. The foot relates to stability as in getting a *foot hold,* or even *getting our foot in the door.* The root word is *ped* where we get words like *pedestal,* something we stand on to express our passionate feelings and ideas. The word *pedantry* means the art of disseminating knowledge, teaching. Pisces has to do with a deep understanding, a deep faith and the urge to get up on a pedestal and share it with humankind.

For Pisces, fulfillment lies in the ability to commune with the god, be that one's art, one's beliefs or the search for unity with all life. Pisces may work in solitude, researching the mysteries of life, painting, singing, calculating or scripting the nature of their heats, but ultimately Pisces will want to bring their gifts to the masses, and to be truly happy, the fishes need an outlet to this end. Pisces can get lost in chaos, lost in the disorganization of endless possibilities. Where the opposite sign of Virgo can become overly ritualized, compulsive in their order, Pisces can become so chaotic they lose the ability to piece the puzzle together. Any occupation that helps them balance between the two would be ideal.

The film *The Fisher King*[15] has many Piscean qualities about it, least of all its title. Here Robin Williams plays Parry, a crazed street dweller in search of the holy grail. When he rescues Jack Lucas (Jeff Bridges) from a suicide attempt turned assault, the two find their lives are inexorably linked. Both each other's victim and savior, they live in a reality confused by Jack's alcoholism and exasperated by Parry's hallucinations. Through blurred boundaries, a spiritual quest, protracted unconsciousness and authentic love, they eventually both find healing and redemption.

Pisces are born when the thought of life reawakening is only a dream. It is a time to contemplate, plan and discuss, a time to research and think towards the future. Often it is like the darkest hour before the dawn and only faith—trust in the unknown future—will lead to the realization of renewal. For Pisces to be fulfilled, he must be allowed to dream, to imagine, to create and to inspire. Through communion with the ineffable, Pisces will find peace.

Part II

X Marks the Spot:
Aptitude Location by House

*T*he houses are like movie sets or stages—raised platforms on which events occur, scenes unfold and acts progress. They can be seen as the backdrop, the arena where a particular event or series of events play out. They represent the ground we stand on in various domains of life.

Understanding the nature of the houses, how they correspond to inner and outer needs, people, places and things, can increase our knowledge of personal talents, aptitude and the *rightness* of what we are best suited to do. Natal activity in a house, or movement by transit and progression, can help us align to what is personally authentic.

The houses are numbered one through twelve and vary in significance according to the individual chart. Some are full of planets and points; some are *empty*. Regardless, each house has a *ruler*, the planet that rules the sign on the cusp, that suggests the most natural approach to the activities described therein. Houses that are particularly important as indicators of aptitude are:

> First House
> Second House
> Sixth House
> Tenth House
> Houses occupied by stelliums (groups of four planets or more)

Houses that contain the Sun, Moon and/or Saturn

Houses containing planets or points within ten to fifteen degrees of the angles[16]

Cadent houses

Houses containing the chart ruler (planet ruling the Ascendant) and the Midheaven ruler

Houses containing the North and South Nodes

Empty houses

Houses being activated by transits, progressions and returns

From this list, it is easy to see that every house can be an important indicator of aptitude. It is a matter of grasping the significance of the individual chart. Each house adds its own insight and information about our needs, wants and desires in any given area of life. The golden rule is: overlook nothing!

It is important to note that *empty* houses are not really empty. Don't think because a house is not tenanted, it has no connection with the rest of the chart or that nothing will happen in that area of life. There is always a house ruler (planet ruling the sign on the cusp) that resides in another house and aspects other planets. The houses also may have less visible occupants, such as transits, progressions or midpoints. Even synastry planets (planets in another person's chart that fall in your chart) can affect any house they fall in. Just remember, there is no such thing as an *empty* house.

Following is a delineation of the houses as they apply to aptitude, talent, resources and natural propensity. Consider the sign on the cusp and any other signs within the house, along with their rulers. Also study any planets or points (Node, Arabic part, midpoint).

First House as an Indicator of Aptitude

The first house, including the rising sign, is of significant importance to uncovering talents and aptitudes in life. The sign and degree on the Ascendant gives the day we were born an individual uniqueness, distinguishing us from the crowd of others. Unhindered, it describes a way of expressing what is natural to us, the path to follow, the map of the journey, the measure of the quest.

Planets in the first house, or rising planets within fifteen degrees of the Ascendant[17] (including those in the later part of the twelfth house) offer their energy to help form our natural way of self-expression. If the eyes are the windows to the soul, the Ascendant is the window through which that soul gazes. It is important to honor the view.

Whatever planet resides in the first house (consider the chart ruler if the house is untenanted) is a key to authentic self-expression. If Mars is in the first house (or Aries or Scorpio is rising) then a certain measure of assertive self-direction is natural. Whether it is the Arian bravado or the contained Scorpionic power, the feeling is one of authority. This individual's natural way, regardless of the rest of the chart, is to initiate and express with force, assurance and vigor. This would feel uncontrived if there were no blocks to expression.

If Venus were found there instead, or Taurus or Libra rising, then the approach would be more subtle and perhaps more seductive. There would be a sense of beauty and allure that might not be present with Mars rising. If both were in the first house, then both qualities would compete for expression. The trick is to recognize and live out the quality(s), in a balanced way no matter how incongruent.

A planet residing in (or entering a house by transit or progression) is *activating* that house in a specific way. Regardless of what the planet represents, it is metaphorically asking the question: *Where am I?* The answer to that, in the first house, is: *I am on my quest.*

The following briefly describes attributes of planets rising in the first house or conjunct the Ascendant. The student will want to build his or her own lists, mentally or manually, creating an extensive array of possibilities for each planet and point.

Sun in the first house: Energetic, flamboyant, warm and robust. This position can give leadership and executive ability. There is a natural flare for distinction, backed by courage and nobility. He may find expression through big business, stage management, acting, consulting—anywhere he can shine. The Sun here says to *strive for significance.*

Moon in the first house: Sensitive, imaginative, nurturing, calculating. This position can lend empathy and the desire to nurture and please. There also is the need to be acknowledged on the feeling level, to contemplate deeply before action is taken. Those with this position may find their empathy expresses in the counseling professions, politics or the caring of others (from landscape gardening to obstetrics). The Moon here says to *honor connections.*

Mercury in the first house: Inquisitive, knowledgeable, changing, observant. This position can give intellectual insights, fluidity and a quicksilver mind. There is a need for stimulation and mental excitement which may be found lecturing, writing, editing and public speaking. Mercury here says *knowledge is power.*

Venus in the first house: Sensual, gracious, artistic, charming. This position can indicate a natural ability to work with the public and in partnerships of all kinds. Mediation is the key. There is a need to associate with and be motivated by others. Creativity may express in all forms of art and beauty from jewelry making to make-up artistry. Venus here says *let's create together.*

Mars in the first house: At home in the first, Mars is assertive, vital, physical, forceful. Mars here needs to declare himself boldly, take risks and assert his sense of healthy aggression. There is skill in initiating plans and ideas, although the follow-through may be left to others. He can be athletic and combative with well-honed competitive skills. Mars in the first says *head's up.*

Jupiter in the first house: Optimistic, enthusiastic, expansive, animated. When Jupiter rises, the world aggrandizes. There is a need to explore, expound and seek the unknown. There is also a drive towards extroversion, custom and pleasure. This planet may express through teaching, lecturing, adventuring or even orthodox religious pursuits. Jupiter here says *turn to me.*

Saturn in the first house: Realistic, cautious, severe, discrete. Saturn here can feel introverted, self-sufficient and mature, giving off a strong sense of sophistication. He is drawn to the sciences, architecture and the building of form with function. This placement achieves success though hard work, determination and self-control. Saturn here says *I can do it myself.*

Chiron in the first house: Scholarly, wise, recluse, compassionate. Chiron here offers wisdom through self-education and can be drawn to the helping professions, occult studies and martial arts. Success comes when the wound is faced as well as the unknown. Chiron in the first says, *I am listening.*

Uranus in the first house: Eccentric, adamant, individual, free. Uranus in the first house wants to express in unique and unusual ways, boasting a sense of individualism at any price. A conformist he is not, nor is he afraid to shock. This placement is adept at leading groups, organizations and expounding on futuristic ideas. There can be an unpredictable quality to the nature, with very sudden shifts and changes. Uranus here says *watch this, if you dare.*

Neptune in the first house: Receptive, intuitive, searching, merging. Neptune in the first gives a sensitivity to life and a longing after the ineffable. There is a quality of knowing more than can ever be articulated. The psychic ability is innate. They need to follow a path that allows for the expression of their gut feelings and desire for oneness with all life. From quantum physics to poetry, the helping professions to music and film, they need to lose boundaries to become who they are. It can get confusing. Neptune here says *merge with me.*

Pluto in the first house: Unwavering, potent, penetrating, reconstructing. Pluto rising in the first brings a measure of intensity that not everyone can handle. They need to deal with issues of power—their own and other's. They need to be on the edge, take risks and meet life with eyes wide open. There is aptitude in all areas that penetrate barriers and unearth things hidden, from x-rays to occult research. Pluto here says *come to the depths with me.*

Second House as an Indicator of Aptitude

The second house is like a gold mine, the store of resources that can sustain us through our life. It may require effort to develop those resources (especially if Saturn or Pluto is there) or it may come with ease (Jupiter or Venus). The thing to remember is that the gold is there.

Traditionally, the second house rules money, finances, possessions that are movable (as opposed to real-estate), what we value and what gives us a sense of security. Because it rules our resources, it indicates our talents and capabilities that can be developed. It also indicates what makes us feel safe and how we relate to the concept of *ownership.*

The signs in the second house, their rulers and any planets or points rising there all indicate what these valued talents and resources are. They are like a list of our assets. These symbols also tell us what to *invest* in to make our lives more secure. Planets falling here ask, *Where am I,* and the answer is *I am in my resources.*

The following brief delineations further describe each planet in the second house and how it relates to aptitude and capabilities. Again, the student is encouraged to amass his or her own list, expounding on these initial representations.

Sun in the second house: Tenacity, stability, desire, sensation. This position can give the ability to amass material possessions and success in the mundane world. There is a natural flare for attracting what they want. They may find expression through fine or performing arts, business big and small, marketing, antiques, construction, architecture—anywhere they can make a tangible show of their efforts. The Sun here says, *This is what I value.*

Moon in the second house: Vigilant, inventive, altering, shrewd. This position can coincide with fluctuations in values, resources and finances. Possessions can be important, bringing a sense of stability and emotional security to the native. If a sense of personal values are developed and matured, the native may rely more on integrity and less on material things. This is a good position for the development of *lunar* activities as a resource: child care, agriculture, culinary arts, banking, bartending, anything to do with water from boating to bottling, women's studies/literature, obstetrics, midwifery. The Moon here says *nurture your own.*

Mercury in the second house: Amoral[18], tricky, brilliant, keen. This position of Mercury suggests that intellect and powers of observation are accessible resources. Siblings and those part-way related may also be supportive. Mercury here can spend time and effort thinking about resources or debating values. This is a good position for mercurial pursuits like communication, writing, teaching, learning, commerce, personnel management and sales. Mercury here says, *I'm thinking about things.*

Venus in the second house: Venus is at home in the second house and here she is luxurious, comfortable, attractive, accumulating. This position of Venus, when unrestricted by conflicting aspects from other planets, coincides with strong powers of attraction. The native usually knows what he or she wants and how to get it. Traditionally, there may be money and resources through inheritance. This position suggests gain and fulfillment through refined and artistic pursuits: gems, jewelry, fine arts, aroma and color therapy, finances, interior design, cosmetics: production, application, surgery. Venus here says *I beautify and acquire.*

Mars in the second house: Adamant, commanding, invigorating, unconditional. When Mars is in the second house, pure enthusiasm and energy can be a great resource. It can spill energy, tangible or intangible, around if in a fire or air sign; it is more contained in earth and water. Financial support can come through Martian endeavors: mechanics, engineering, conflict (from martial arts to the law) athletics, surgeons, physiotherapists, drummers, leaders, sculptors in metal, tattooists, sheep farmers. Mars here says *follow me.*

Jupiter in the second house: Prosperity, wisdom, enriching, enchanting. Jupiter in the second house can bring a sense of wealth and optimism to the individual, regardless of his or her station in life. Confidence and a bright outlook are great resources here. It can also coincide with a philosophical approach to life. Resources can be attracted through Jupiter pursuits like teaching (university or higher levels) travel (agencies/guides), advisors or counselors of all kinds, attorneys, financiers, publishers, editors, clergymen (women), celebrants, and work of any kind with large animals. Jupiter here says *I can be anything.*

Saturn in the second house: Garnering, persistent, retentive, focused. Saturn in the second house of the natal chart suggests that talents, resources, finances, possessions and personal values are all going to carry a big charge. Where Saturn is by house is the area of life we feel most vulnerable, where we compensate for ours flaws and where we face, eventually, our fears. It is the house of hidden treasures, once those fears are resolved.

Saturn in the second traditionally was associated with austerity, although it shows up in the signs of millionaires often enough. The underlining theme is the pursuit of tangible security along with the ease and peace of mind that comes with sharing resources with others. Those with Saturn here need to work hard to build their stockpile, be it monetary or theoretical, and then use it to encourage and support others.

The development of Saturn-associated talents is necessary. This can be accomplished by pursuing occupations and activities like science (especially archeology, paleontology and orthopedic medicine), building and construction, engineering, architecture, mathematics, government work, chiropractic, debt collection, real estate, teaching and organizing of all kinds. Saturn here says *get to work.*

Chiron in the second house: Intuitive, self-reflecting, contentious, healing. Chiron in the second house can indicate an aptitude for intuitive thinking, empathy and inner strength. There is a quality of wisdom here, although it must be developed and nurtured for the greatest result. This placement needs time alone for inspiration and understanding.

Chiron can be developed through the study of the occult, astrology, fine arts, applied sciences, psychology (all kinds of therapeutic and counseling fields), communications technology, teaching, (special or higher education), physiotherapy, rehabilitation and physical training disciplines like weight training, martial arts, gymnastics, yoga and individual sports. Chiron here says *learn, empathize and discover.*

Uranus in the second house: Insightful, unpredictable, progressive, unique. Uranus in the second house suggests a roller-coaster ride where money and finances are concerned, as well as some unusual or offbeat talents. There is a desire to explore and shock. With this placement, banal and mundane pursuits are definitely out. Uranus requires the development of individuality and genius.

Some talents and aptitudes associated with Uranus include information technology, computer graphics and animation, electronics, sound engineering, electronic or computer generated music, astrology, numerology, the occult, abnormal psychology, space travel, social work (humanitarian pursuits), kinetic energy, inventions, neurosurgery, photography, psychology, psychiatry, physics, union activities and rocket science. Uranus here says *dare to be who you are.*

Neptune in the second house: Mystical, trusting, empathetic, beguiling. With Neptune in the second house, the immaterial is the greatest support. Too much emphasis on materialism can lead to material loss. The paradox is that often the material is seen as the divine and this placement can be associated with great amassing and subsequent loss. The focus has to be on honesty, because deceit, intentional or not, leads to ruin.

Neptune in the second requires the development of high values and integrity when dealing in the financial world. The more egalitarian, the better. Talents and resources include aptitude in the arts, music, mysticism, anesthesiology, medicine, psychology, marine studies of all kinds, secret humanitarian societies, poetry, literature (romantic, fantasy) the film industry, drama, work in institutions, detective work, addiction counseling, hydraulics, the occult, poison control, spiritual aspirations and anything connected to water. Neptune here says *seek what is lasting.*

Pluto in the second house: Survival, temptation, power, force. With Pluto in the second house, money, finances and values can be wielded like a sword of truth. Values may be based on *either/or*, black or white, until deeper shades of gray are discovered. This position suggests the need to develop a personal sense of power and authority as opposed to relying on other's. There is a distinct need to be on the edge, physically or emotionally, by creating risks of all kinds.

Talents and aptitudes include ambulance and rescue work, emergency medicine, crisis counseling, atomic energy, chemo and radiation therapy, radiology, pandemic medicine, sex therapy, undertaking, special forces agent, disaster specialist, the occult, criminal justice, dangerous/poisonous animal handling, tax investigation and politics. Pluto here says *find what is hidden.*

Third House as an
Indicator of Aptitude

The third house is the seat of consciousness. It represents what we think and what we think about what we think. The operant word is *think.* This house bustles with activity, mental and physical, and represents all forms of communication by travel, thought, telephone, FAX, e-mail or post.

Traditionally, the third house rules our early education and environment. It has to do with short (familiar) journeys, siblings, neighborhood, taken-for-granted skills, memory, perceptions and speech. It also indicates how we learn, teach and communicate in the world.

The signs in the third house, their rulers and any planets or points rising there all indicate how we go about communicating, thinking and relating mentally to others. Honoring them—finding ways and means to express our intellectual side authentically—means living a more fulfilling life. When planets falling here in the third house ask, *Where am I?*, and the answer is, *I am in my head.*

The following brief delineations further describe each planet in the third house and how it relates to aptitude and capabilities. Again, the student is encouraged to amass his or her own list, expounding on these initial representations.

Sun in the third house: The Sun in the third house says *teach.* This doesn't necessarily mean becoming a traditional teacher; it means honoring the need to communicate no matter what the occupation or pursuit. The emphasis is on conscious knowledge—learning and sharing ideas. The topic itself is secondary.

This position may be fulfilled by developing language, interpretation, writing, lecturing, speaking and signing skills. The medium of communication may range from radio announcing to personal consultation, lecturing to tour guide. The important thing is to seek knowledge and share it with others.

Moon in the third house: The Moon in the third house can turn thoughts into imaginative dreams and wistful fancies. People with this position of the Moon learn more by absorbing knowledge from others than enrolling in traditional courses or programs. It is not a reflection on their intelligence; it is more a statement of the natural approach to information gathering. This position learns most by listening to others.

To feel at home, comfortable and nurtured, the Moon here needs change and stimulation. There is a restless quality that can get bored easily with routine and predicable schedules. The Moon here says, *If you love me, give me an interesting, stimulating environment with people to talk with and places to go.*

Mercury in the third house: Mercury is at home in the third house and here it is a natural researcher. In its home domain, Mercury here wants to gather knowledge, teach skills and work with detailed bits of information. They may have strong ties with one or more of their siblings and want to work with them as adults.

Because the investigative skills are strong, this placement is good for any diagnostic occupations, trouble shooting, undercover inquiry or detective work. There is a distinct need for new events and avenues to unleash the ravenous curiosity. Mercury here says *let me communicate the information I have discovered so all can be illuminated.*

Venus in the third house: Venus in the third house expresses a pleasing, artistic and refined quality in their thoughts and communication skills that can charm allies and adversaries alike. Because there is a propensity towards persuasion and enticement, they make good diplomats and mediators.

This placement expresses itself best in right brain, creative pursuits. Unless there is a strong Saturn contact, they may not have the drive and perseverance for extensive academic programs. Music, art and dance need a place in their lives, even if this configuration belongs to a rocket scientist. Venus here says *show me your ideas and I will turn them into art.*

Mars in the third house: Mars in the third house loves a good verbal dispute. This placement can have a habit of acting before they speak, speaking before they think. Sometimes their decisions are made from a place of impulse and have strong repercussions.

The energy of Mars doesn't want to be trapped in the mind and is constantly looking for ways to express in the physical world. Those with this placement may want to vent their excess energy through the body in athletics, yoga, martial arts or solitary sports like running or swimming. Once channeled, the energy of this sign can be associated with powerful, innovative thinking, leadership qualities and abundant energy to drive a project or initiate new ideas. Mars in this house says, *take me to your leader and I will talk him into anything.*

Jupiter in the third house: Jupiter in the third house expands the landscapes of the mind and is associated with mental optimism and a rich camaraderie with family relations. The intuition is strong and, if trusted, the king of the gods in the third house can bring luck through being in the right place at the right time with the likelihood of saying all the right things.

The most important thing to acknowledge with Jupiter here is the considerable mental restlessness that comes with the placement. The occupation needs to provide enough activity, challenge, stimulation and movement to keep this planet happy. If it is lacking, the energy can scatter along with all the big plans and the awesome ideas. Jupiter here says, *the bigger the idea, the better the outcome.*

Saturn in the third house: Saturn in the third can indicate a potent mind, although it may feel more like a brick wall than a vast horizon at first. Young people with this placement may feel *stupid* or inadequate and find the early school years very difficult. Often there is an interruption of schooling, undetected dyslexia or other challenges that set the individual up for a seeming *fall*. What does come with this placement is a mandatory need to develop the skills of thought, communication and expression, no matter how difficult, bad or painful that process may seem.

Through hard work, early dysfunction and fear can turn to brilliance. The ability to pursue the most challenging projects, stick with long term ideas and produce results at all odds are the rewards well earned although there are demons to face before this is achieved.

Saturn here is not likely to work with siblings or relatives and may find itself spending long hours alone, writing, programming, organizing, preparing. This is an acute mind with unfathomable depths, if time is taken to plumb them. Saturn here says, *not without struggle will you understand.*

Chiron in the third house: Chiron here corresponds to a curious mind that seeks fluctuates between involvement within the community and retreat from that involvement. It is hard to be just one thing. Occupations that require full and constant social interactions without a break are just as unauthentic as ones that require total reclusion. Chiron is the messenger between the two and needs to keep one foot in each world.

Those with Chiron in the third may be attracted to areas of research or academics that require solitude followed by public exposé. They may enjoy a teaching schedule that allows for times of research and study. They may work in the field of martial arts or yoga, disciplines that require retreat from daily activity. As long as Chiron has time to meditate as well as communicate, the results can be fulfilling. Chiron here says *just when you think you have it, I will show you another way.*

Uranus in the third house: Uranus in the third house electrifies the mind and brings a whole new meaning to the term *excitement.* This is the mind of the rebel, the progressive thinker and the pursuer of unique ideas. There is tremendous mental energy that needs to be used if the nervous system is to avoid burnout.

Ideas come suddenly to those with this placement and they need to keep their lives as spontaneous as possible so they can act when lightening strikes. Aspects to Saturn can help ground the concentration in practical ways. This placement is ideal for the self-employed, director, leader or executive that answers only to themselves. Occupations that allow for the most freedom and flexibility suit best. Uranus in the third says *ignore my inspiration at your own risk.*

Neptune in the third house: Neptune in the third house links to a deep and rich imagination. The creative skills are strong, although often not traditional. Because Neptune tends to blur boundaries, traditional study programs can be challenging. These people don't think, learn or concentrate in the predictable or conventional ways.

Regardless of the chosen profession or occupational pursuit, this placement needs to express its extreme creativity and poetic flare. They understand the belief behind the wisdom, the meaning inside the purpose. Knowledge can become like a deity, guiding them into the depths of their own inspirational wealth. Neptune here says *believe what I know.*

Pluto in the third house: Pluto in the third house has something profound to say, and those with this placement need to listen to the call. Whatever they do, there can be a life and death urgency to the expression of thoughts and ideas. It goes without saying, this placement is intense.

Pluto here may be a teacher, though not in the traditional sense. The individual may write books, although the topics are unlikely to be mainstream. There is a deep need to express something to the rest of the world and anything that supports and develops the ability to do so brings them closer to fulfillment.

Mental conflicts, power struggles and out and out family fights (especially with siblings) are all symptoms of the need to experience the gripping intensity and power that Pluto desires. Finding creative ways to encounter such fervor is helpful to reaching goals, expressing feelings and making a living through the written and spoken word. Pluto here says *knowledge is power*.

Fourth House as an
Indicator of Aptitude

The fourth house represents the depths of the soul. It has more to do with *what* we are than *who* we are. This house is often associated with shadow contents of the unconscious because the orientation here is not always easy to express in daily life. These qualities may be repressed and then subsequently projected onto others (to which we will respond with strong and sometimes extreme emotions). The fourth house is often subtle, but never weak.

Traditionally, the IC and corresponding fourth house rules home, family, ancestors and genetic inheritance. It has to do with our experience of the parents, particularly the father or *hidden* caregiver, and anything that surrounds and protects. There is an emotive content here not found in the first three houses because the fourth is ruled by Cancer and its planet, the Moon. Feelings run deep in this domain, and past experiences may be triggered by current events making reactions strong and accentuated.

The signs in the fourth house, their rulers and any planets or points rising there all indicate how we go about setting up a home, responding to and creating a family, buying property, building a house and relating to parents. This is the place where we keep things hidden, sometimes even from ourselves.

The fourth house also rules how we end things—relationships, jobs, obligations, contracts, feuds and projects. The sign on the cusp and the planets contained within all offer clues to how we approach this area of life. Planets falling in the fourth house are *accidentally* dignified because of their angular position. This gives them added significance. When they ask, *Where am I?*, and the answer is, *I am in my dwelling*.

The following brief delineations further describe each planet in the fourth house and how it relates to aptitude, capabilities and inner emotional needs. Again, the student is encouraged to amass his

42

or her own list, expounding on these initial representations.

Sun in the fourth house: The Sun in the fourth house can indicate a strong need to *shine* as a unique individual within the family or on the home front. This may present a struggle because the family background can be strong and influential, difficult to break away from. They may prefer to work from the home as opposed to venturing out into the world. If they do venture out, there is a tendency to make their workplace as *homey* as possible.

This position of the Sun indicates a person who does not want his or her life to be on view. Privacy is very important and so is confidentiality. They may go to great lengths to hide themselves in some way, or maintain a duel or secret life. They may also go to great lengths searching for just the right place to settle down and build a home. Wherever they decide, they need to be king of their own castle, master of their own domain.

This placement can indicate a nostalgic side to the personality that is in strong evidence in the early years. They may be attached to their childhood home, parents or an idealized version of how wonderful things were *once upon a time*. There may always remain this undercurrent of longing, no matter where they live as adults.

Aptitudes here include the ability to work on their own in the home studio/office, an acute sensitivity to movements in the collective (artistic trends, hunches and ideas) and situations that require self-sufficiency. The need here is to establish strong foundations in the world along with a sense of emotional stability. This is often easier to achieve as life progresses. The Sun here says *only by the depths shall you see me.*

Moon in the fourth house: The Moon in the fourth house resides in its natural domain. Here self-nourishment and self-protection can be a strong motivating force. There is a love of home as sanctuary, a place to revitalize and retreat.

Fluctuations in emotions, home (moving house or moving country) or in the occupants of the home can accompany this placement. There is a natural restlessness that needs the peace of seclusion from time to time. There is also a natural need for cyclic change in the domicile and the emotive turmoil that leads to growth and renewal.

The Moon is at home in the fourth house and those with this

placement can feel comfortable in lunar occupations involving ancient things, research into the hidden or occult, archeology, real estate and welfare. Psychic sensitivity may be strong as well as the intuitive *gut* feelings. The Moon here says, *you enter my heart when you enter my home.*

Mercury in the fourth house: Mercury in the fourth house can indicate a restless soul that needs stimulation, challenge, movement and opportunity to feel emotionally stable. It is a paradox. There can be may changes of residence although whether this causes anxiety or not will depend on the aspects to Mercury, the fourth house ruler and the general tone of the chart.

This placement can benefit from a creative career that allows and facilitates the expression of ideas, feelings and needs. Without this, the native may become tense and hypercritical, especially on the domestic front. It is not always easy for them to say what they mean and encouraging this ability leads to feeling of contentment. Mercury here says *I know what you are thinking; can you say the same of me?*

Venus in the fourth house: Venus in the fourth house can coincide with loving attachments to the home and family, and if not heavily aspected by outer planets, a positive experience with relationships there. The angular position strengthens Venus and can suggest an affinity for social activity and a natural interest in people.

Occupations that bring others into the life are more authentic than ones that may isolate the native. There is also a refined sense of creative expression in the depths of the soul that needs to be nurtured to feel complete. Venus here says *lift the veil and feast your eyes!*

Mars in the fourth house: Mars in the fourth house represents potent energy residing at the roots of the being. Those with this position need to develop a sense of self-will and self-direction that may mean breaking away from the domination or control of the father, parents or family line.

Natives may feel more at home in active, energy demanding occupations that allow them to be boss. In subservient endeavors, they can become tense, emotive and disgruntled. Mars here needs to call the shots on the home front. He says *there is a battle ragging in the unseen depths.*

Jupiter in the fourth house: Jupiter in the fourth house can bring optimism, generosity and confident potency to the base of the native's emotional stability. There may be a natural trust and enjoyment in life that embellishes everything they do. These people often find success in the vicinity of their birth place, or at least in their own country.

This placement can indicate an inheritance or benefit from the family line. There is a sense of support there that helps the individual progress through life. Jupiter here says the home must be spacious. This is a reflection on the deep soul need for freedom and expansion innate with this placement. Jupiter here says *the scope of my soul is eclipsed only by starry heavens in the night sky.*

Saturn in the fourth house: Saturn in the fourth house can be a tremendous source of strength, but not usually right away. The early home life may have been austere, emotionally or pragmatically, and the native may be left with a feeling of oppression around family, feelings, parental relationships and worthwhile outcomes. They may strive ambitiously to better their position, financially if not emotionally, goaded by a sense of disappointment perpetrated often by the father.

There is a deep soul desire to be self-sufficient, to not have to rely on someone who may, sooner or later, let them down. This placement can cut one off from life, especially as the years progress, and needs continuous attention if it is to blossom. What is this blossoming? It is the enrichment that comes from an inner self-confidence and self-containment that can also make and keep symbiotic relationships with loved ones. There can be a great sense of personal responsibility as they learn not to blame or manipulate. These things will not come without effort.

This placement indicates strict or severe influence from the home and family, and those with Saturn here can benefit from getting away from the early environment—striking out on their own. Saturn here says *by my own strength and in my own time shall all be accomplished.*

Chiron in the fourth house: Chiron in the fourth house can indicate a deep need to mediate. There may be a natural skill in communication, empathy and psychic ability. People with this placement need to build bridges, bringing seemingly opposite energies together.

Sometimes there is a family wound or secret that comes to light, giving the native an opportunity to heal some long perpetuated damage. Often it is through a sensitivity to the father or an experience of abandonment that this will happen. Chiron here can also indicate powerful compassion that is effective in the healing or counseling arts. He says *seek me in my seclusion, in the quiet of the night.*

Uranus in the fourth house: Uranus in the fourth house electrifies the soul and symbolizes a deep need for stimulation and change. This is not a placement that tolerates ruts or routines. There can be an unconscious desire to disrupt any stable situation if complacency threatens. Those with this placement may have trouble applying themselves to long term commitments because of a deep seated fear of stagnation.

It is possible that the early home life was erratic, leaving the native with a sense of instability at his or her roots. This person will need a vital occupation, one that involves change, travel and unexpected and unforeseen events. Anything dealing with information technology, astronomic studies, astrology and digital arts (film, animation, effects, sound engineering) may attract these individuals because they have an aptitude here. Freedom and self-will are very important once they break free of family ties. Uranus here says *spontaneity is the gift of life.*

Neptune in the fourth house: Neptune in the fourth house can indicate potent spiritual longings at the depths of the soul. There may be a sense of loss through the father or other caregiver that never seems to be appeased until the native finds a spiritual source within. The individual may have endured addictive or alcoholic parents, or mysterious skeletons in the family closet.

Here the need is to find an inner sense of union with the divine that does not involve addiction, co-dependence, guru seeking or lopsided relationships of any kind. Core sensitivity is strong and so are creative and artistic skills. Through expressions of their inner landscapes and a sense of union with the divine, these individuals can find peace. Neptune here says *seek fulfillment in the depths of your soul, not somebody else's.*

Pluto in the fourth house: Pluto in the fourth house can indicate a potent family inheritance, sometimes akin to a family curse. There is great power as a resource for these individuals, although they may have to face many demons before that power can be owned and wielded.

The early home life may have felt dangerous, as if the very survival was threatened. The father or other caregiver may have felt extremely omnipotent, a hard act to follow. Sometimes there can be a deep brewing well of unresolved feelings bubbling underneath the surface.

Pluto can indicate a raw, primordial nature and, in that respect, those with this placement may flourish in jobs that deal with the harshness and mystery of mother nature, such as the applied sciences, marine biology, anthropology, archeology, psychology and the occult. If nothing else, this placement indicates a deep and eternal store of courage, fortitude and strength to face the darkest adversary. Pluto here says *here lies the treasure: enter at your own risk.*

Fifth House as an Indicator of Aptitude

The Fifth house represents the joy and nature of the heart. It has to do with our sense of creativity—creative self-expression—and the way we go about engaging a feeling of uniqueness. This is the area of life where we want to feel acknowledged for our special creative talents.

Traditionally, the fifth house rules artistic expression (drama, theater, fine arts, music, dance, visual arts, sculpture, literature) speculation, children and love affairs. These are all areas of life that can make us feel distinct, honored, loved and admired. Relationships belonging to this house center around those with lovers, children and children of the mind (artistic projects). Its natural sign is regal Leo, ruled by the brilliant Sun.

The signs in the fifth house, their rulers and any planets or points arising there all indicate how we go about expressing our creativity, falling in love, having children and taking chances. When planets reside in the fifth house ask, *Where am I?*, and the answer is, *I am in my heart.*

The following brief delineations further describe each planet in the fifth house and how it relates to aptitude, capabilities and inner emotional needs. Again, the student is encouraged to amass his or her own list, expounding on these initial representations.

Sun in the fifth house: The Sun is at home in the fifth house and here it shines light on the powers of creative self-expression. Those with this placement need to develop their creativity, regardless of the medium, in order to understand who they are. The need is to be distinct, either through children of the mind, body or heart.

If this placement is not honored, then inexplicable depression can set in. The joy of the heart—through love affairs, books written, pictures painted, dances choreographed, scores sung or plays performed—must be expressed. Occupations or hobbies that enhance and support this creative drive are essential. For that reason, the Sun in the fifth can fit professions that involve the arts, theater, drama, radio, film, television and performance of all kinds. Since this placement naturally wants to be the center of attention, all positions of leadership apply. The Sun here could also be involved with children in a creative, facilitating way. This placement of the Sun says *play with me in the dance of life.*

Moon in the fifth house: The Moon in the fifth house has less *will* for distinction than the Sun and more of a drive to go out and enjoy the sights. This is a pleasure-loving Moon that finds romantic liaisons, arts shows and theatrical pursuits nurturing. There can be a strong attachment to their children and a need to feel nurtured by them.

The Moon here has all the creative flare of the Sun in this house. The difference is that the Sun often has to work for it; the Moon not necessarily so. Being creative, having children, engaging in love affairs, even betting at the races, all have a natural, relaxed and nurturing feel for this Moon.

A fifth house Moon can carry a natural charm that appeals to the public without aim or effort. Unless the Moon is challenged by harsh aspects or in an uncomfortable sign, this artist may or may not make a profession of his or her craft, but each will feel at ease creating and others will notice. The Moon here says *shall I wave my magic wand?*

48

Mercury in the fifth house: Mercury in the fifth brings the bright and curious intellect into the realm of creative expression. There can be strong linguistic skills, as well as an aptitude in literary arts. Communication can become a form of art, expressed in the spoken or written word or through the body in dance.

Any creative challenge that requires mental wit and agility is at home here as are physically precise activities like yoga, team sports or equestrian events. This is a strong placement for those who teach young people, especially adolescents. Mercury here says *meet me on the playing field!*

Venus in the fifth house: Venus in the fifth house needs an outlet for its creativity, regardless of the chosen occupation. These natives will not be completely fulfilled without it. If those with this placement feel unbalanced or stressed, the pursuit of an artistic avenue can recreate equilibrium. Whether they paint, dance, write or sing, be it music or drama, culinary arts or 3D graphics, they need to express it in the world, simple as that.

If this placement is not nurtured, the desire to create may be projected onto others—especially partners or offspring—regardless of the other's aptitude or desires. Once aware of this misplacement, the native can find ways to cultivate his or her own creative outlet, taking the pressure off the child or partner. The more their creative skills are integrated into the career, the more fulfilled they will be. Venus here says *resist me at your own demise.*

Mars in the fifth house: Mars in the fifth house brings a lot of energy, competition and power into the field of self-expression. Those with this placement need to express in a creative and dramatic way to feel a sense of self-will and self-direction. Natives with this Mars may be in high-risk occupations, competitive sports or other aggressive activities, or in a position of authority in a creative project or pursuit.

This is not a placement that can take a back seat in a group or partnership endeavor. These people need to be the boss or at least have some artistic control. Conflict can arise when this is not granted, as in a case of the musician with a large controlling record company or an actor with an ambiguous contract. Mars here says *battle please!*

Jupiter in the fifth house: Jupiter in the fifth house can be expansive in its creations, having a *bigger is better* approach to every-thing it does—large murals, big productions, huge showcases. Fortunately, these natives often seem to do no wrong. There is a natural sense to what will bring success, and natives with this place-ment can also gain from financial or real-estate speculations.

The key to Jupiter here is the feeling of joy that creativity can bring. It's natural and necessary. This planet of expansion says *if you aren't in it, what is the point?*

Saturn in the fifth house: Saturn in the fifth needs to create ev-ery bit as much as Jupiter here, although the desire may be cruelly ignored, thwarted or squashed. Where Saturn is by house is where we must go to retrieve a vital piece of ourselves, and in the fifth house it is a piece of our creative hearts. Saturn may have to work very hard at expressing to glimpse it.

Sometimes this placement indicates a native who makes a job of his or her creativity, turning pleasure into task and demand. With Saturn, the need is for both creative expression and structured work. This can translate into occupations that teach art, especially to youth, or explore some of the harder physical aspects of creativ-ity, such as dance, large-scale sculpture, exacting stage perfor-mances and the organization or administration of these fields.

The thing about Saturn is that it can mean doubt. It is a place where we feel flawed or deformed and the hesitancy to expose that disfigurement is understandable. The paradox is, we must in order to feel fulfilled. Saturn in the Fifth is *Beauty and the Beast* com-bined and how can we love a beast we have never let out into the light of day? Saturn here says *take up the burden of your creative destiny.*

Chiron in the fifth house: Chiron in the fifth house can build a bridge between the collective desire to create and the faculties to do so. This can be the placement of an art teacher, art therapist or any-one who works creatively with others, especially children and youths. Chiron here may find ways to heal the self or others through the world or creative self-expression. He says *do not fear the ter-rain written in your own body.*

Uranus in the fifth house: Uranus in the fifth house zaps into the creative, heartfelt world like an electric live wire in the mid-dle of a storm. There is no subtlety here. The will is strong, the

50

intention is direct, the ego well reinforced. These can be extremely creative types, although they are never mainstream, never traditional.

Uranus here wants freedom to express creative ideas in unique and unusual ways and these people bring a flash of newness, a vitality, to any project they work on. It is important to acknowledge that they need to be their own boss. Group work is fine as long as they are in command. This is not a subservient placement. Uranus here says *in the unusual is revealed the profound.*

Neptune in the fifth house: Neptune in the fifth house can make a deity of the creative arts. There is a need to let the artist inside *sing,* no matter what the medium. These individuals have the capacity to tap into the collective and produce literary works, visual arts or performances that set the populace on fire. It is not done because they want to; it is done because they must.

As with any of the outer planets in the fifth, creativity is a vital part of the life that must be lived out in some way if the native is to feel fulfilled. Here the imagination is as potent as the ability to act out many different dramatic roles. Challenges arise when they feel they have obligations to others that keep them from freely pursuing their own desires. There can be times of great sacrifice and also great artistic expression. Through sacrifice and suffering, the artist, if he or she survives, softens and emerges. Neptune here says *to find peace you seek the art.*

Pluto in the fifth house: Pluto in the fifth house brings with it great power, authority and focus. It also brings some challenges where ego identification is involved. Self-importance can get out of hand or, conversely, be buried so deep no one can find it. Those with this placement may find that creativity is accompanied by dramatic upheaval, conflict and trauma, although in the end the creation always seems worth it.

Where Pluto resides, issues of power erupt, and here it may be in the art world, through working with children or offspring or in the field of competitive speculation. The need is to develop a sense of authority through mutual respect and integrity. With this placement, creations always come from the depths of the soul. Pluto here says *through the descent will the artist and lover be reborn.*

Sixth House as an
Indicator of Aptitude

The sixth house represents the ritual, day-to-day routine of life. There is a sense of commitment in this house, be that to an employee, a boss, one's body, pets and the ways and means we get things done. It has to do with our sense of power to manifest what we want. Here we make ourselves psychosomatically healthy or psychosomatically ill. Our relationship to those that serve us and those we serve is portrayed by this house.

Traditionally, the sixth house rules ritual magic in its capacity to manifest. It also rules employment, pets, health and gadgets. Howard Sasportas said, *The sixth house is all about sticking to our plans and blossoming into precisely what we are meant to be.*[19] This is the landscape of daily living that compares the inner nature of our lives with the outer. It brings together psyche and soma, body and mind, inner spiritual life and outer reality. If things don't mesh, we become sick, depressed, apathetic and ineffectual. Aligned, planets here can be the key to a basic sense of well-being. When planets falling in the sixth house ask, *Where am I?*, the answer is, *I am in my daily rituals.*

The following brief delineations further describe each planet in the sixth house and how it relates to aptitude, capabilities and inner emotional needs. This house is particularly important, because if we are not happy in out routine daily lives or employment, we are not happy at all. Again, the student is encouraged to amass his or her own list, expounding on these initial representations.

Sun in the sixth house: The Sun in the sixth house suggests the need to provide service and ritual routine in order to discover the nature of the Self. Those with this placement can have a strong urge to connect the body with the mind in everything they do. These are the bridge-builders between inner being and outer manifestation. They may strive to fashion their identity around health, work and routine. The focus can be on a physical or psychological challenge that they may spend a lifetime unraveling.

This placement of the Sun demands a working relationship with the body, be it through health diets, exercise routines or physiotherapeutic endeavors. In some way, the Self must serve the body. Any career avenues that support this premise—body workers, physical therapists, health professionals, psychologists who link psyche to soma, dieticians, herbal therapists, aroma therapists, sports medicine professionals, athletes, veterinarians, nurses, writers or teachers in these fields—will help give the person with a sixth house Sun a stronger sense of self-fulfillment.

The practice of the occult in its ancient and ritualized forms, the development of a refined craft or simply obtaining skills that lead to gainful employment are also ways and means to develop the Sun here. The need is to work, to develop and to connect. The Sun in the sixth house says *through the web of ritual order do I shine.*

Moon in the sixth house: The Moon in the sixth house suggests that emotional stability and contentment comes from routine tasks, work and ritual. There is a need to keep things organized to feel safe, secure and nurtured. *There is nothing as clean as a witch's kitchen* sums up this position nicely when considering how much psychic dross can cling to the corners and windows of a house. The Moon in the sixth is particularly sensitive to these forms of *left over* energy and will do its utmost to cleanse them.

This placement brings a sense of the nurturing mother to the daily life, whether there are children to rear or not. The job can become a place to express these maternal needs or it can be where we look to have these needs for nurturing fulfilled. Occupations that allow for a sense of closeness and family, blood or otherwise, are important as this position prefers not to work alone, at least not all the time. The Moon here says, *if you love me, work with me.*

Mercury in the sixth house: Mercury is at home in the sixth house and here it can bring a sense of restlessness to the daily routine that needs change, stimulation and interaction. The drive is to obtain knowledge and information, and the matrix is in the daily living. Here Mercury is the messenger of the gods, connecting information from the body to the consciousness and back. Learning to listen to those words of wisdom can help bring about a feeling of well-being. Watching for signs, omens and synchronicity can bring deeper understanding.

With this placement of Mercury, the life work needs to be mentally stimulating and physically activating as well. If the job is sedentary, those with this Mercury need to take up hobbies that counterbalance physical stagnation. These activities might include yoga, gym, dance, swimming, running or horseback riding. If, by contrast, the work is physically active but not so much mentally, they need to involve themselves in a research project, reading club or other intellectual pursuit. Mercury here says *insight comes through ritual order.*

Venus in the sixth house: Venus brings a blessing (if not harshly aspected) wherever it falls, and in the sixth that benediction can be on the health of the body or in the pleasantness of day-to-day living. Venus attracts a sense of popularity at work, and is often associated with good conditions all around. It can also have some amorous fascination with coworkers, employees and lodgers, adding excitement and/or drama to the daily routine!

This placement can indicate talents in arbitration, mediation, women's issues and health. There is a natural ability to bring people together and formulate an agreement. Whatever occupation is pursued, Venus here suggests the ability to sharpen skills and develop natural talents easily. There is an intrinsic artistic competency that may express in fitness, health and beauty. This can extend into interior design, architecture or any work that requires exactitude. The only caution with this placement is the propensity for overindulgence in delectable things, on and off the job. Venus here says *find the beauty in routine.*

Mars in the sixth house: Mars in the sixth house brings the warrior to the workplace. This placement suggests the need to assert a sense of healthy aggression, to be self-directed when it comes to day-to-day living and routine. In the house of service to others, that can spell *trouble.* The sixth house indicates how we get along with those above and below us in the chain of command, yet when Mars isn't on top, it gets cranky.

The planet of war likes to *push* and than can mean a push to work harder, lift more weights, eat stricter diets, do more tasks and win more battles. With no reprieve, the body can become exhausted. All that energy needs to be directed at nurturing the body and balancing the routine if one is to stay healthy.

Mars in the sixth prefers to work alone, and be its own boss. It can also mean that the *push* is directed toward protecting coworkers, bosses, employees or those less able to defend themselves, such as abused animals or children. Mars here says *seize the day!*

54

Jupiter in the sixth house: Jupiter in the sixth house expands the landscape of the daily routine. Nothing is mundane and dramatic events can be a rich source of nourishment. Where Jupiter falls is where we like to mythologize life. In the sixth house, that means our day-to-day living.

Ideally, Jupiter placed here has the opportunity to serve others. Jupiter is an organizer, a facilitator, mediator and benefactor. He likes the wide, sweeping view, and can instigate programs of reform, education, travel, spiritual development, health and well-being. Jupiter brings support, and in the sixth that means sustenance, livelihood and the ability to manifest needs, goals and desires.

Jupiter searches for meaning and in the sixth house that meaning must come from the daily routine of living, the work they do and their ability to be of service to others. The health is strongly connected to the sense of purpose, and if illness or disabilities arise, looking at the situation symbolically can be of great assistance to recovery. Jupiter here says *I expand the daily horizons.*

Saturn in the sixth house: Saturn in the sixth house may work very hard to create order in routine daily life. Those with this placement can focus on work under exacting circumstances, although they tend to expect others to match their strength and concentration. They can be critical when others, or themselves, fall short. This placement coincides with a great deal of demand, internal and external.

Aptitudes here include administrative abilities and strict attention to detail. Saturn wants to create order, yet in the sixth that order can turn to regimen. There may be a fear of chaos, a fear of loss of boundaries that puts this placement on constant guard.

Where Saturn resides is where we meet our shadowed selves, the flaw and the wound. In this house that wound can be exposed at work, through interactions with coworkers and during any routine activity—washing dishes, having a dental checkup, jogging in the park. The key is to face the beast wherever it arises and gain some understanding and insight into the depths of the shadowed self. Through work, ritual routine and day-to-day living, this may be accomplished. Saturn here says *build the body; hoist the load.*

Chiron in the sixth house: Chiron in the sixth house sends a particular message about linking the body and the mind, psyche and soma. Any planet here has this purpose, although Chiron may state it the loudest. With this placement, the body and the soul mirror each other in every aspect of daily living.

Whatever the occupation, there is a distinct need to incorporate a philosophy that bridges what goes on in the psyche with what goes on in the body. Unusual physical attributes may come up with this placement, along with correspondingly unique mental or psychic anomalies. Whether they work within the body-mind-spirit vocations (helping professions, counseling, herbal medicine, chiropractic, body work, massage, neo-Reichian therapy, the occult, martial arts, dance therapy) or follow more traditional pursuits like teaching, technical trades or traditional medicine, those with Chiron here will benefit from exploring this great link. Chiron here says *teach, learn, connect.*

Uranus in the sixth house: Uranus in the sixth house demands a routine that never gets old! There is an innate need for change, stimulation, innovation and originality. Commitment is difficult only when it presents itself as a restriction of the moment, idea or potential. Uranus here never wants to get into a rut!

There is an aptitude for anything technologically innovative—computer programs, information technology, new methods of communication as well as the fields of astrology, psychology, health, social welfare and education. These people can be a touch willful and impatient and, as such, work best as directors or supervisors as opposed to employees. They don't like being told what to do!

This placement can be severe and will benefit by the development of empathy and understanding. It is important to remember that Uranus anywhere abhors routine and it may unconsciously create upheaval and drama in the life to keep the banal at bay. Finding work that fills the need for freedom, stimulation and surprise will bring feelings of fulfillment to enrich the life. Uranus here says *seek surprise in every new day.*

Neptune in the sixth house: Neptune in the sixth house can bring a fog of confusion to daily life. It is challenging for this planet of the ineffable divine to lodge easily in the realm of the body and day-to-day living. All sorts of unusual things may manifest: obscure illness, hidden agendas, hypersensitivity at work, psychic sensitivity arising during routine tasks. No wonder people with this placement become confused!

It is said that confusion is a sign of *wrong goals* and with Neptune here wanting everything one moment and nothing the next, it is no surprise things get a bit mixed up. This placement indicates tremendous sensitivity for which the individual may not be prepared.

Neptune in the chart is like a psychic sponge, absorbing feelings, emotions and agendas like a thirsty blotter. In the sixth, that means the daily routine tasks of life, health routine (or lack of it), foods eaten, work and coworkers, and even pets can be a source of psychic input. It is important to choose carefully in these matters.

Those in occupational environments that are destructive may become physically ill because of the sensitivity there. If the daily routine is fraught with dilemmas, the diet poor, exercise limited, it can manifest as problems with the body if it remains unacknowledged. Conversely, this sensitivity can be used as a resource in daily life, particularly in occupations that work on an intuitive level: counseling (especially addictions and eating disorders) medicine and healing (traditional or alternative) or artistic endeavors (acting, visual arts, film, writing, poetry, music). The key here is to learn to function inside the order of the environment and the body without losing contact with everything else. Neptune here says *find the divinity in details.*

Pluto in the sixth house: Pluto in the sixth house brings the power of transformation into the workings of daily life. Sometimes it can feel like heating a pot of tea with a nuclear reactor. Overkill.

Pluto likes to make a life and death matter of anything in its domain and in the sixth that can mean choosing a pet food, dressing for work or sweeping the path. It is the little ordinary things that bring or trigger profound change.

Pluto has to do with power and authority—how we dish it out and how we receive it. In the sixth, experiences of this nature are likely to crop up at work. Who is the boss and how does that person handle authority? Those with this placement best prepare to address these issues on a deep level.

Aptitudes associated with this position of Pluto include the ability to command (or the need to learn what that means), a penetrating (x-ray) vision that perceives the meaning behind words and actions and a rash desire to live *on the edge*. Pluto here can excel in the area of detective or research work of all kinds, medicinal and healing arts, psychology, politics, and occupations that deal with the power of nature (firefighters, disaster/rescue teams, explorers and scientists). Pluto in the sixth also has a proclivity toward the occult mysteries. In this house Pluto says *take risks daily*.

Seventh House as an Indicator of Aptitude

The seventh house represents our personal one-to-one relationships and committed partnerships. This is the area of life where we push out from ourselves and join forces with another. Sometimes it is a place of contest, as in dealings with the court, adversaries and open enemies. Sometimes it is a declaration of recognized union as in marriage or legal partnerships. Whether friend or foe, this house portrays our acknowledged relationships in life.

It is important to note that although the seventh house traditionally represents the *other*, it is still a house in our own chart. Think of the seventh then as qualities inside us that we tend to project onto others and then relate to them as if they were *not us*. This is the mirror on the wall that looks like someone else, yet reflects only ourselves.

Understanding aspects of the seventh house can help us learn more about our inner attributes and how we may respond to partnerships, business associates and people with whom we enter into contracts. Some planets here can indicate a positive approach to contractual associations and others argue challenges that must be met if success is desired. As an angular house, all planets falling here are *accidentally dignified*. When planets in the seventh house ask, *Where am I?*, the answer is, *I am in my open relationships*.

The following brief delineations further describe each planet in the seventh house and how it relates to aptitude, capabilities and inner emotional needs. Again, the student is encouraged to amass his or her own list, expounding on these initial representations.

Sun in the seventh house: The Sun in the seventh house symbolizes a person who needs relationships to discover the meaning

58

of Self. These individuals do best in partnerships that provide a sense of relating, as well as growing uniqueness. There can be a tendency to want to hold the power in a partnership or, conversely, give up that power. Either way leaves this individual unbalanced. The development of a natural give and take is essential.

The Sun here can gain a feeling of distinction through joint ventures and activities because working with another highlights one's own individuality by contrasting it with someone else. These people can make great business partners when the seventh house Sun is working consciously.

If the Sun is in difficult aspect, there can be another story. Father issues, troubles with authority figures or a desire to project one's own solar identity onto a special, idealized other can crop up. Conscious awareness is required here, or partnerships turn into workshops for the identity challenged. The Sun here says *through relationships, I discover who I am.*

Moon in the seventh house: The Moon in the seventh house makes a home of relationship. There is a potent and sometimes unconscious sensitivity to others that understands their needs and how to nurture them. This can be the lunar position of someone who really knows how to please the public. Often this Moon suggests a person who does not want to be alone, making the individual adaptable to partnerships of all kinds.

The catch is that where the Moon falls by house is where we experience fluctuation and change. Those with this placement may find it challenging to maintain a stable working relationship without taking on the identity of mother, caregiver or sensitive, moody creative type. Conversely, moods and instability may be projected onto the other person, leaving him or her to live out the psychic content of the individual. These issues need to be contemplated deeply prior to the signing of contractual agreements. The Moon here says *through relationships, I nurture and sustain.*

Mercury in the seventh house: Mercury in the seventh house wants to build a bridge of communication between the Self and the partner. There is a need to gather, sort and impart information in an open and trusting way and those with this contact can do well in partnerships in the communications field, education or information technology.

A difficult placement here can bring challenges through documents and legal contracts where something has been misrepresented, intentionally or unintentionally. There should always be a careful scrutiny of material before signing, and detailed communication prior to a sealing handshake. Mercury here says *through relationships I move and express.*

Venus in the seventh house: Venus is at home in the seventh house and this can indicate a natural affinity toward partnerships. If the goddess of love is well aspected, there can be much success in these joint endeavors. There can also be the challenge of keeping sensuality out of business relationships because the powers of attraction are strong here.

Venus can be at ease in all kinds of social situations, offering a sense of harmonious grace and receptivity. This is a strong placement for those who work with groups of people, society and the public, and mediation, diplomacy and management of all kinds. People skills come to life in rich settings such as the art and fashion world. Venue here says, *through relationships I discover my inner values.*

Mars in the seventh house: Mars in the seventh is a bit of a contradiction of terms. Here we have the drive for independence, aggression and self-will in the house of relationship to the other. The dilemma between the two can be crippling. How can we get our way and be the boss and still enjoy the benefits of union, business or otherwise? Mars in the seventh demands we figure this out.

Mars here can dash headlong into a partnership without giving it due thought. It can also warn against legal difficulties, arguments and trouble in general with partnerships. Forewarning aside, Mars can function in the context of relationship if certain considerations are made.

Mars is severe. It wants to take control and be the boss. To function in a healthy relationship, this drive has to be balanced with a sense of empathy and compassion for the other person. Too little Mars, however, is just as impaired because the individual would then lose his or her capacity to act authentically and assert his or her will. This position may suggest that although Mars is not a natural team player, it has a lot to learn from the experience of one-to-one relating. There can be energy and initiative in abundance. Mars here says *through relationships, I triumph.*

60

Jupiter in the seventh house: Jupiter in the seventh house can indicate a sense of success in all matters related to partnerships, especially those of a legal nature. There is the natural Jupiter optimism and social adaptability that can make these people well liked and sought after.

Often where Jupiter is in the chart indicates where we find support and encouragement. In the seventh, that can mean the partner offers support, believes in the other person and makes things happen that would not have manifested without them. Jupiter here can enter into partnerships that involve teaching, travel, legal studies and ceremonies of all kinds. The *greater benefic* in this house says *through relationships, my vista expands.*

Saturn in the seventh house: Saturn in the seventh makes work of relationships and implies that, although sometimes terribly difficult, relationships are the key to self-fulfillment. Where Saturn falls in the chart is where we feel damaged, weak or crippled and here in the seventh it is personal one-to-one relationships and business partnerships that bring out the beast.

This doesn't mean partnerships should be avoided. On the contrary, it is vital to form them, learning and discovering deeper layers of the Self along the way. Isabel Hickey said of Saturn in the seventh: *Not good for partnerships in business if Saturn is afflicted. Lone wolf type who does better alone but he doesn't learn as much.*[20] The challenge here is to learn to relate symbiotically with another in business or pleasure.

Saturn wants to be self-sufficient and in the seventh that creates a quandary. Cooperation may not come easily, yet it is important for these individuals. They have to acknowledge a deep fear of becoming dependent or overly involved—the fear of being vulnerable to another—and learn to embrace a healthy and mature relationship. Saturn here says *through relationships I meet my shadow within.*

Chiron in the seventh house: Chiron in the seventh house can indicate an attraction to or partnership with someone involved in teaching, healing or mind-body pursuits like martial arts. There can be an aptitude for empathy that makes those with this position strong counselors or therapists.

Relationships can have a healing quality when Chiron is found here, as if through working together both parties are made to feel more whole or more complete. This may not manifest until after about age twenty-six, when Chiron passes by transit through the first house. Chiron here says *through relationships my destiny is met.*

Uranus in the seventh house: Uranus in the seventh house can mean unpredictability in partnerships or at least a desire for excitement. This is a classic position for a *freedom vs. closeness* dilemma that can play out in the form of an independent partner always pulling away or a needy partner always clinging tightly. The important factor to remember here is that if we have this configuration, both expressions belong to us. We want to be both close and free and it takes a lot of awareness and emotional maturity to live it out in any balanced way.

Business partnerships need to be entered into with great awareness. There can be sudden, unexpected events that bring windfalls as well as downfalls; the native must be prepared for either. Expect the unexpected and the out of the ordinary to occur. Boring is one thing this placement is not. Uranus here says *through relationships I shock, stimulate and inspire.*

Neptune in the seventh house: Neptune in the seventh house can idealize relationships, living a dream that is destined to eventually pop against the sharp points of reality. This can be a tricky position for business partnerships as misunderstandings or outright deceptions can occur. Direct communication, honesty and integrity are vital for any successful co-ventures.

Neptune here can be a martyr to a mate, taking on more than its share of the necessary sacrifices. Eventually, the individual might grow to resent it. Expectations and assumptions need to be abolished. A partnership can not function honestly or smoothly with these foes tagging along. Neptune here might be highly sensitive to movements and trends in the collective and any occupation that tunes into these feelings—music, fashion, pop art, film, literature—can benefit. The healing arts and service to those less fortunate can also fit this signature. The key is to stay grounded and above board with all those involved. Neptune here says *through relationship I seek the divine.*

Pluto in the seventh house: Pluto in the seventh house can indicate rash power struggles with business partners or those involved in joint projects. This doesn't mean relationships of this kind should be avoided. It means that great awareness needs to be placed on the issues and dilemmas that surface when signing on the dotted line.

Pluto wants to feel intensity, power, survival and merging. It wants to plummet to the depths of the unconscious and dig for the treasures buried there. In the seventh, these needs of the god of death must be met in personal one-on-one relationships. Those with this placement may find it healthy to have several *primary* relationships—romantic, business, therapeutic, creative—to spread the energy out. Otherwise Pluto has only one kitchen to cook in and that can make a pretty big fire. Pluto here says *through relationships I meet my soul.*

Eighth House as an Indicator of Aptitude

The eighth house represents a kind of erotic merging with others. This is Eros in the Greek sense of the word, where two or more people come together in such a way that they create a lasting transformation—sometimes this happens sexually, but not necessarily so. The eighth house also rules the occult, other people's finances and death—all areas of life where we have to give something up with no guarantees of the outcome.

In terms of aptitude and talent, a strong eighth house can indicate an ability or need to take risks, delve deep under the surface and merge our energy with others to create something new. Areas of interest could range from researchers, accountants, tax officers, bankers, investment analysts to those who study the occult, psychology, or are involved in shared intimate experiences of any kind.

Understanding aspects of the eighth house can help us learn more about how we handle true intimacy and trust. This is particularly important when working with others, business or otherwise. However it unfolds, it will not be superficial. When planets falling in the eighth house ask, *Where am I?,* the answer is, *I am in the depths of my soul.*

The following brief delineations further describe each planet in the eighth house and how it relates to aptitude, capabilities and inner emotional needs. Again, the student is encouraged to amass his or her own list, expounding on these initial representations.

Sun in the eighth house: The Sun in the eighth house symbolizes a person whose identity is derived from working on an intense and intimate level with others. They need to go to the *edge*, take risks and work without guarantees or expectations. It is the sense of faith, the leap in the dark, that wants to be evoked. Anything risky and complicated is intriguing for those with the Sun here.

This placement also suggests the need to support and facilitate others in some way. They may involve themselves with occupations that encourage other people's creativity in teaching, coaching, promoting and publishing. This Sun can also bestow a hint of the taboo on the essential nature, making anything off limits fascinating or even irresistible. The Sun here says *through merging with others my identity shines.*

Moon in the eighth house: The Moon in the eighth house may be deeply sensitive to the undercurrents of those around it, personally and collectively. This may translate into the ability to sense developing trends from fashion statements to fluctuations in the stock market. This would obviously be a good placement for those working in speculative markets or industries that rely on a *gut* instinct to sense impending shifts and changes.

Where the Moon is by house is where we want to have our emotional needs met; in the eighth that means intimacy that creates transformation. There can be an aptitude for nurturing other people's talents, abilities or finances. Developing these innate skills will bring a sense of joy and fulfillment into the life. The Moon here says *nourishment comes through intense intimacy.*

Mercury in the eighth house: Mercury in the eighth house wants to communicate on a deep and meaningful level. Superficiality is out; dark secrets, taboo experiences and hidden meanings are in. This is the mind of a researcher, detective, occultist or investigator of any kind.

Those with this placement have something profound to say, teach or write. It may be done on a small, family or community level, or it may take on global proportions. Either way, the seriousness of this placement must be honored or it could degrade into a propensity to spread destructive gossip or rumors. Mercury here says *intensity and risk bring out the expression in me.*

Venus in the eighth house: Venus in the eighth house attracts other people's money through inheritances, legacies or business transactions of one's own instigation or through a legal partner. These individuals need to be able to work with others intimately and deal with the day to day problems that can arise when money and finances are involved. Psychic abilities are strong.

Venus here can also indicate an easygoing side to the nature that could get so relaxed they rely totally on the support of others for subsistence. With such strong abilities to attract the trust, interest and finances of others, it would be a shame to let this go to waste. Venus here says *I relate through intense intimacy.*

Mars in the eighth house: Mars is at home in the eighth house and here he awakens in the sphere of sex and death. The risks they like to take are just a little riskier and the relationships they like to have are just a little more intense. There is nothing passive or lackadaisical about Mars in this house. Sleep is the last thing on his mind.

Mars here give the power to assert, to take action based on a gut feeling, to compete financially and take breathtaking risks. There can be difficulty though sharing the profits, and disputes can arise over joint finances, partnerships, contractual agreements and wills or legacies. Discipline is required in all these areas for Mars to be a success. The god of war here says *my passion awakens in the fires of intimacy.*

Jupiter in the eighth house: Jupiter in the eighth house is like a guardian angel that looks after the native through other people's resources. This can be through financial contributions or in more subtle ways of emotional support, encouragement and psychic strength. Again, intuition is potent here; acting on a *wild hunch* more often than not brings gain.

This placement is usually very good at handling crises or undo amounts of stress. There is an ability to see the big picture and they can transmute that confidence to others during difficult times. Occupations that require faith, depth, risk and a cool head are good areas to explore. Jupiter here says *through merging with others I grow and expand.*

Saturn in the eighth house: Saturn in the eighth house makes the exploration of the inner world a necessity. This may be resisted for many years, yet at some point the native will turn to deeper matters of life and of death. There are issues around intimacy because this placement can bring great fear and longing for transformational merging with another. The dread may socially isolate people or it may overcompensate by thinly spreading the passions. In either case, intimacy is missed, avoided and escaped.

Business partnerships need careful handling with this placement because matters of trust, honesty and generosity can arise. Joint resources can be a problem when it is hard to give and receive. Because this area is so important to the native, he or she can work hard in the field of finance, business partnership and shared resources, psychology, death and occult studies, making a career out of an otherwise challenging area of life. Through helping others manage their resources and merging with them, financially, psychologically or emotionally, Saturn in this house brings illumination and fulfillment. The god of the Titians here says *true intimacy turns the Beast into Beauty.*

Chiron in the eighth house: Chiron in the eighth house can live out as a teacher or messenger of occult knowledge. These natives may develop themselves in unique ways in the fields of psychology, mystical studies, astrology or even disciplined physical pursuits such as martial arts, dance and yoga. Always there is a theme of intimacy, risk and merging. The need is to communicate something from the deeper side of life. Chiron here says *through intimacy the wounds of others heal.*

Uranus in the eighth house: Uranus in the eighth house likes to crack open mysteries, taboos and secrets with the blaze of a lightening flash. There is nothing subtle here. Those with this placement may tend to act impulsively in the area of business partnerships and joint finances, although deeper investigation is always recommended.

The intuition is potent with this placement and, although there can be unexpected challenges with business finances, there can be unexpected windfalls as well. There is strong interest and aptitude in the deeper studies of nature manifesting in anything from astrology, alchemy, magic and psychology to nuclear physics, telepathy and psychic experimentation. These people may use information technology in new and exciting ways. Uranus here says *risk the depths and soar through the heavens.*

Neptune in the eighth house: Neptune in the eighth house can indicate an aptitude for helping others develop themselves artistically, emotionally, psychologically and financially. Often this is done with little or no gain for the native. If the service is provided with a generous heart, the results are their own reward.

When the goal is strictly financial accumulation, Neptune in the eighth can go sour. There can be complications, deception, confusion and misrepresentation around contracts, business plans and joint partnerships. Those with this position need to exert caution in selecting a partner, joining a co-venture and entering mergers. There is always a risk, although Neptune's healing, empathic and psychic abilities are strong with this placement. When developed for the service of others, they can be very fulfilling. Neptune here says *intimacy leads to the grace of the divine.*

Pluto in the eighth house: Pluto is at home in the eighth house and the god of death can plunge the native into the intensity of the underworld through a connection with profound issues of sexuality, aggression and power. This is not a lightweight placement and natives with Pluto here may want to explore this side of human nature through creative channels such as crisis counseling, law enforcement, emergency medicine, emergency rescue units and working with the dead or dying.

Pluto here demands that we deal with power and authority, risk and aggression, taboo and sometimes treachery. Meeting this challenge head on, through a chosen path or career, can be the quickest way to working with this energy. Conversely, if it is ignored, Plutonian violence, power confrontations and brushes with death seem to happen at will, leaving the native feeling powerless, frightened and overwhelmed. This placement strongly suggests that the bull be taken by the horns. Pluto here says *enter the depths and be transformed.*

Ninth House as an Indicator of Aptitude

The ninth house takes us beyond the ordinary day to day boundaries of life to expand our possibilities. It involves anything that broadens the horizons: foreign travel, higher education, meditation, spirituality, philosophy and orthodox (but not necessarily dogmatic) religion. This is the area of life where we search for and construct a belief system that gives us a strong sense of meaning and purpose.

In terms of aptitude and talent, planets in the ninth house can indicate an ability or need to amplify life, expand the horizons and go for new possibilities. There may be strong inspiration and spiritual vision. The drive is to travel to the unknown, be it areas of the mind, body or spirit.

Certain planets here, especially near the Midheaven, can be an indication of career path, mission or profession. They are in no way weakened by the cadent house position. The ninth is also associated with teaching (especially university level), the law, ceremony, publishing, exploration, foreign matters, clergymen and in-laws. When planets falling here ask, *Where am I?*, the answer is, *I am in my vision.*

The following brief delineations further describe each planet in the ninth house and how it relates to aptitude, capabilities and inner emotional needs. Again, the student is encouraged to amass his or her own list, expounding on these initial representations.

Sun in the ninth house: With the Sun in the ninth house, identity can be gained through the development of talents in the area of understanding. This includes higher education, philosophy, information technology, religious leadership and publishing. These people have a message to deliver and this placement of the Sun needs to find a way to deliver it.

This house deals in abstract ideas, concepts, beliefs and visions. There is interest in foreign cultures, myths and rituals, and these themes may be integrated into the profession, no matter what it is. The capacity to understand and translate deeper meanings is inherent here and the development of this talent can bring greater fulfillment in life.

This placement is also associated with organizational management and coaching skills, imbibing enthusiasm and confidence to any goal or adventure. Whether lecturing, writing, publishing or organizing travel adventures, this placement of the Sun get joy out of sharing its knowledge and wisdom with others. The Sun here says *through exploration I find myself.*

Moon in the ninth house: The Moon in the ninth house loves to travel, discover new territory and experience new things. There is comfort and nurturing gained from a belief system that lends meaning and purpose to life. This placement can be strongly intuitive, instinctively understanding symbolic messages in signs, synchronistic events and dreams. There can be a natural association with a foreign country through the mother or family. This Moon may indicate a foreign residence at some time in the life.

Talents here include anything that caters to the public (the Moon has an uncanny sense of what the collective needs), writing and publishing. There may also be an aptitude for politics because this placement may be involved in government, large and small. The Moon here says *exploration into the unknown brings nourishment.*

Mercury in the ninth house: Mercury in the ninth house, with its strong interest in communication, is a natural teacher. The messenger of the gods comes into his own here, disseminating information, inspiring thought and provoking new ideas. This placement can take a step back, view the larger patterns and discover a greater understanding.

Endeavors that allows for this kind of inspiration include writing, publishing, travel, reading, philosophy, religion or spiritual pursuits, education, diplomacy, law and public relations. The aptitude lies in the curiosity, inquisitiveness and desire to learn and communicate. Mercury here says *through exploration I gain knowledge and insight.*

Venus in the ninth house: Venus in the ninth house may feel *the grass is always greener on the other side of the fence.* This placement loves to travel away from the place of birth—in mind, body or spirit—and may well reside far from the original *home.*

There is interest and ability in foreign diplomacy, mediation and cultural studies. There can be a sense of peace and ease gained from a solid belief system that offers spiritual support and security in life. Those working in the creative arts tend to express their particular philosophy of life through their work so that others may benefit or understand. Venus here says *beauty is found in the unknown.*

Mars in the ninth house: Mars residing in the ninth house brings energy and potency to the inherited belief system and view of life. Those with this placement may come from a zealot background and become dogmatic or fanatical themselves if they're unaware. There is much energy and conviction. They can also feel they need to break away from a traditional religious system and assert their independence in this area of life.

Travel may be embarked upon spontaneously, as sudden plans and adventure opportunities arise with challenge. Knowledge and experience can give those with this placement a sense of power and authority. Careers that offer a chance to expound on these talents include the ministry, teaching, publishing, high ranking military officers, executives, company directors, and athletes (captains, coaches and owners of). Mars here says *exploration gives me strength.*

Jupiter in the ninth house: Jupiter in the ninth house resides in its home and hearth and augments the natural love of travel, philosophy, education, symbol, belief and meaning. There is a strong aptitude in these areas of life, and the individual with this placement could find success in the fields of travel, publishing, higher learning and writing. They make fine public speakers if there are no other problematic aspects.

Too much of a good thing, however, can be fanatical. Jupiter here can be so absorbed in its own thoughts and beliefs and goodness that any action can be justified, as if it came ordered directly from the divine. This kind of excessive confidence, under containment, can sometimes be an ally in the field of the performing arts for actors, artists, musicians and politicians. There is certainly talent in this area of life, along with writing, publishing and mediation. Jupiter here says *the broader the horizon the greater I become.*

Saturn in the ninth house: Saturn in the ninth house can symbolize individuals that harbor the fear of God in the depths of their soul. There can be a strong religious inheritance that must be faced if they are to develop their own authentic philosophy and beliefs in life. Finding that true faith is paramount with this placement.

Saturn here may not be naturally comfortable with flying, extensive travel (unless associated with work) or too expansive of boundaries. There is a need to contain spaces, ideas, philosophies and beliefs in life. There can be cynicism instead of hope, criticism instead of support. Too much room can give them the jitters; it can also be a goad to deeper understanding and inner comprehension. When Saturn in the ninth comes to terms with its God, laws, beliefs and meanings, there can be tremendous strength in the ability to discover inner truths. These people may have an aptitude for all sciences (particularly physics) medicine (human and veterinary), philosophy, theology or metaphysics. Travel, university and mediation may never be completely fun, although it can be very productive for those with this placement. Saturn here says *the gold is buried in the well of meaning.*

Chiron in the ninth house: Chiron in the ninth house can show strong aptitude in areas of education and higher learning. The natural propensity to teach comes into its own in the ninth house, describing the lecturer, professor and dean of faculty. Other areas of capability include astrology, philosophy, applied sciences, human movement and healing. Chiron here says *learn and I will astonishment you.*

Uranus in the ninth house: Uranus in the ninth house brings the sweeping air of change to belief systems. There is a super-charged search for the meaning of life that can knock over anything and everything that gets in its way. The goal is to discover the truth; the stage is the unlimited universe.

This placement indicates a unique and unorthodox view of religion, education and expression of philosophical ideals. Their vitality and enthusiasm for *the search* can make for stimulating conversations and travel partnerships, although there can be difficulty settling down with any belief for long. The chopping and changing can be challenging for others of a more steady nature.

Aptitudes lie in the field of science, invention, innovation and exploration. They make stimulating educators, writers and publishers, although they can sometimes be too bombastic for foreign affairs. Where Uranus falls is where we seek stimulation and vitality and in the ninth, the sky is the limit. Uranus here says *the search will lead to new and unexpected meanings.*

Neptune in the ninth house: Neptune in the ninth house can indicate a lifelong search for meaning, a kind of divine homesickness for which there may be no permanent cure. There is a need to find expiation through religion or a belief system which can lead to involvement with cults, religious bodies, gurus and spiritual masters.

The problem here can be that if one finds a master, the only other opening is for a disciple (or slave). Projecting the numinous onto a ninth house figure is possible here. Ultimately, people with Neptune in the ninth need to discover a union with the divine inside their own higher self, irrespective of the mortals that inspire them.

Some of the Neptunian search for meaning can translate into extraordinary philosophy, art, music, theater, film or dance that is searched for or expressed worldwide. On a practical level, this placement of Neptune can sometimes manifest as confusion or fogginess around the path of higher education, and overseas flights and travel in general can be fraught with misunderstandings and mistakes. Here, Neptune loves to meditate and can have strong psychic abilities. The god of the mysterious seas in this house says *expand your boundaries to seek the numinous.*

Pluto in the ninth house: Pluto in the ninth house wants to discover the depths in the nature of life, the meaning of the universe and the existence, if not intentions, of the divine. There can be a ruthless pursuit of this mission, or, if other conditions indicate, a ruthless denial. Pluto never experiences things in halves, and if we don't think we can take it, we desperately attempt to shut it out. Of course, a denied Pluto is usually much more dangerous than the one you invite to dinner.

This placement can coincide with dogmatism, fanaticism or any sort of extreme belief, philosophy or religion. It can also indicate a person who has had to extricate himself or herself from a family inheritance of fanatical control and manipulation. The successful result of this kind of battle speaks for itself in terms of the personal attributes of strength, power and self-direction.

Where Pluto resides in the chart is where we meet the ruler of the underworld, the depths of our inner selves. In the ninth, this can happen through higher education, teaching, discussing philosophy or traveling to a new and unexplored destination. Those who handle this placement well can be very adept at articulating deep inner turmoil, making them excellent teachers, counselors, writers or editors. They often have something of high impact to communicate, and will take great risks to do so. Pluto here says *for each decent into the unconscious another fair world will arise.*

Tenth House as an
Indicator of Aptitude

The tenth house traditionally represents public standing, career, mission, profession and social identity. Not so much an indicator of aptitude, this is more a sign-post for how the innate talents and abilities may be used in society. Certainly, those with planets and points here will have a strong public face. What that face looks like depends on the planets, their aspects and destiny of the individual.

Planets in the tenth house can indicate our interactions with society and, if not the actual profession, our approach to it. The drive here is to be seen (or not seen) in the world in a particular way, as suggested by the nature of the signs and planets found there. Any planet in the tenth tends to attract public attention, opinion and even sometimes scandal. How the individual feels about the attention will depend on the planet(s) involved.

The Midheaven is a very important point that needs to be honored and lived out if we are to feel fulfilled in life. If someone has Leo on the Midheaven and the Sun in the tenth house, he or she is never going to feel accomplished in a behind-the-scenes occupation. This is not a support person, homemaker or gaffer. Conversely, someone with a Virgo Midheaven and Neptune there may work behind the camera, behind the scenes, and feel full contentment doing so.

It is important to consider the sign and ruler of the Midheaven, its ruler's placement and any planets residing in the tenth. When planets falling here ask, *Where am I?,* the answer is, *I am in my vocation.*

Sun in the tenth house: When the Sun reaches the apex of the chart in the tenth house, the world becomes a stage. The need for acknowledgement and social recognition is intricately woven with the search for Self. The person with this placement blossoms as an individual when the drive for significance is nurtured. It is best they don't hide.

The Sun in the tenth house wants to deal with issues of power and authority. They do best in a command position, pursuing a career field that reflects their Sun sign and aspects. This could be in any area of life; the important things would be their sense of leadership and control, and level of public significance. The main pursuits in life would need to have practical results, offering something of benefit or profit for themselves or others. If the Sun is not too heavily aspected, those with this placement have the discipline and honor to reach great heights, whatever their chosen field. When the placement presents splits and challenges, they may achieve those heights in the face of great adversity. The Sun here says *by my calling do I find distinction.*

Moon in the tenth house: The Moon in the tenth house has a natural sense of significance. These individuals are acutely sensitive to the general population and can intuitively know how to please and nurture them. Any career pursuit that uses this ability can bring success.

Where the Moon falls, things fluctuate and the Moon in the tenth can mean changes in career path, occupation or even reputation and public image. This can be the politician whose notoriety alters with a turn of events or the firefighter that turns to marine biology or starts a market garden and then runs a chain of hotels. This position evokes emotional situations through the mission or profession, encouraging the native to feel life as well as do it. The Moon here says *through my career(s) do I feel nurtured.*

Mercury in the tenth house: Mercury in the tenth house, unhampered by challenging aspects, is the natural speaker, writer and public addresser. This is an individual who can communicate thoughts and ideas to society at large. Any occupation that involves the written or spoken word—from teaching to publishing, writing to information technology—to anything that transports (people or information) from one place to another is comfortable here.

There is a natural curiosity about life with this placement that spills over into the vocation. This Mercury is often seen by others as intelligent, articulate and dexterous. Anything that helps to develop these qualities will enhance the feeling of fulfillment in life. With difficult aspects to Mercury in the tenth, there may be a struggle to get the word across and communication can be arduous. Still, any planet in the tenth needs to shine and will do best if encouraged to express, no matter what the challenge. Mercury here says *it's only my calling if it expresses what I think!*

Venus in the tenth house: Venus in the tenth house can indicate a light, breezy and friendly approach to the world. There is a natural feeling of prosperity that goes along with this placement, often bringing success and recognition in an easy and unfettered way. Even with difficult aspects, Venus here can turn on the charm in social and public situations.

This placement often projects a sense of grace and refinement that attracts others and gets desired results. Any profession involving the arts—visual or performing—diplomacy, fashion design or modeling, beauty care or makeup artistry, certain kinds of personal one-to-one counseling or body work, and theoretical law can suit. Venus here says *refinement of the calling brings success.*

Mars in the tenth house: Mars in the tenth house brings the god of war into the career, mission or profession and it doesn't like to just stand around quietly. Ambition can be strong, as is the sense of self-authority. These people generally need to be their own boss.

People with this placement are often seen as powerful, authoritative and dynamic. They like to climb to the top, meet challenges and fight for success (the worse the odds, the better). Mars likes a good confrontation and any career pursuit that allows them to struggle and win can be fulfilling. This can range from military commanders to martial artists, sales representatives to professional athletes, auto mechanics to fire fighters. Mars here says *give me mission impossible!*

Jupiter in the tenth house: Jupiter in the tenth house expands the vocational horizons and gives a great desire for achievement, success and a positive public image. The king of the gods is on display here, and always likes to look good.

This placement can indicate a need to maintain a high level of integrity to assure positive public standing. Any career that puts them in the limelight—law, corporate business, film and theater, politics, banking, education—can fulfill this need. There are no guarantees, however, that they will never be caught in a compromising position, the details of which are spread from cover to cover of all the tabloids.

This placement can also indicate an interest in international travel and connections, broad-based communications, acting, philosophy and religion. Some may pursue the advice and presence of a teacher or guru, and others may become one in their own right. Jupiter here says *the calling will constantly expand!*

Saturn in the tenth house: Saturn is in its natural house in the tenth and needs, more than anything, to achieve a sense of honor, recognition and public position. This ambition may be fraught with fears of failure (what if I'm not good enough?) fears of success (what if I succeed and I'm still not happy?) and feelings of being laid open by the public (will they see my vulnerability?). It's enough to make us run away and hide for the first three or so decades of life.

In spite of, and often because of, the trepidation around vocation and social image, Saturn here can indicate the greatest success of all the placements. There are just a few hills to climb and challenges to meet before it happens. Foundations must be built on solid ground, step by step. There is no skipping a rung in the ladder, no windfalls that make it easy. Saturn chooses the hard and high road, and people with this placement need to evoke the power and humility to follow.

These individuals need to be seen as self-sufficient and competent by society. Anything they can do to back up their chosen career with degrees, authentication and certificates will help. Anything from business to medicine, science to teaching, architecture to the law can suit this placement. The key is hard work, integrity and acknowledgement of a healthy ambition. Saturn here says *face the Beast and meet your glory; ignore the Beast at your own ruin.*

Chiron in the tenth house: Chiron in the tenth house, like Saturn, may not be sure where to fit into society, although instead of developing the ambition, Chiron is likely to develop qualities of service, communication and healing. There can be interest in alternative medicine, therapies, body work (chiropractic comes from the root work *chiro*, meaning *hand)* martial arts, astrology, occult studies and herbal medicine. Chiron here says *not just any career will do.*

Uranus in the tenth house: Uranus in the tenth house brings electric insights, upheaval and change into the landscape of career, mission and profession. There is a potent individualistic streak that needs to be self-employed, independent and in charge. The ideas may be original, even genius, although they may be stubbornly fixed. Boredom comes easily.

Those with this placement will benefit from exploring the pro-

76

gressive and extraordinary things in life, using intuition and energy to develop new ideas, ways and means of doing things. They need to be doing something meaningful and will not tolerate well a rut or routine around career or vocation. Restlessness is strong. They require a lot of stimulation to hold their interest.

Pursuits that involve computers, information technology, programming and design, astrology, social welfare, politics or anything unusual, stimulating and different suit this position. The key here is freedom, challenge, animation and movement. Uranus here says *awareness through revolution.*

Neptune in the tenth house: Neptune in the tenth house can expand the career possibilities to such far reaches, blurring them so extremely, that the native doesn't know what to do. Confusion around career can be a challenge in the early part of the life, to say the least. It can take some years before the native settles into his or her life work.

This is a good position for any vocation that gives more than it receives. The healing arts, medicine, humanitarian pursuits, the arts (writing, music, poetry, dance, photography, performance) and work in institutions with those wounded or victimized can be authentic and rewarding. Sometimes this placement becomes involved in politics, film or other positions where the individual becomes *famous.* Where Neptune is in the chart is where we meet the divine, and in the tenth that means in society, career, mission or profession.

Those with this placement need to be on guard against shady or corrupt associations. Neptune culminating can point the finger at who will take the fall if things go wrong. Circumspection is required. Neptune here says *pursuit of the mission leads to the divine.*

Pluto in the tenth house: Pluto in the tenth house insists on a vocation that is deep, intriguing, dangerous, meaningful and potent. There is no half way. Pluto in the tenth needs to be on the edge, take risks and deal with the raw, intense and ruthless side of life.

Some with this placement will pursue careers that deal with the powers of nature. Firefighters, disaster rescue workers, space explorers and miners fall in this category. Others will deal with issues of power and danger in the fields of big business, medicine, depth psychology or the occult. If they write, they will explore the darker nature or transformational recess of human experience. If they paint, their images will reflect their vision of the underworld. If they perform, their roles will deal with power, authority and the primordial side of human nature.

Whatever they do in society at large, they bring Pluto with them. Finding creative ways to honor this god of the underworld will lead to the riches promised there. Pluto in the tenth says *find success through power and introspection.*

Eleventh House as an Indicator of Aptitude

The eleventh house traditionally represents our relationships to those in a group or organization. If the seventh house is seen as personal *one-to-one* relationships, the eleventh house can be dubbed the domain of *one-to-many.* This is also the area of life where our goals and objectives for the future are defined. Here we strive to become everything we can possibly be.

The eleventh is the house of friendships, camaraderie and hopes and wishes for the future. It describes what can make us happy and which aspects of ourselves we need to encourage to experience that sense of happiness. The eleventh can describe the types of groups we gravitate toward, the friends we make and the nature of our future desires.

Entering the eleventh house is like walking into a collective web where we experience a connection with the rest of our species. In terms of modern physics, this is the interconnection between all life, and those with planets here can feel it keenly. This is a group consciousness that melts the ordinary boundaries of pragmatic living and views them in a holistic, interrelated sense while still maintaining a distinct identity. Social awareness may be strong and planets here can illustrate how we relate to friends and society. When planets falling here ask, *Where am I?,* the answer is, *I am in my collective.*

Sun in the eleventh house: The Sun in the eleventh house gains a sense of self-awareness and individuality from being part of the group. These people may be leaders or work closely in the ranks; the important thing is to be an integral part of the group.

This placement can indicate a strong association between friends and success. Goals and objectives may be reached with the help of friends or associates, or they may gain most in life by being a friend. The person with this placement works best with others, avoiding long bouts of isolation or retreat.

Aptitudes and talents associated with this house include the field of social welfare, humanitarian endeavors and political pursuits. Those with this placement may find themselves working in a group or team situation in anything from rock music to scientific research. There can be a natural gravitation toward group therapy (leading or participating) or a propensity to support and encourage the career of friends. The Sun here says *I shine brightest in the company of like minded others.*

Moon in the eleventh house: The Moon in the eleventh house can be a hallmark of those who seek comfort and nourishment from the fellowship of friends (especially female), groups and organizations. There is a strong sensitivity to the consciousness of the group, and people with this placement can be easily swayed if there are no strong, independent aspects to the Sun or Mars. Aptitudes here include an acute awareness of the mood and feelings of the group, benefiting those involved in therapy, politics, public and motivational speaking and education. This placement can indicate fluctuating goals and wishes for the future that need focusing. The Moon here says *friendships and associations bring nurturing.*

Mercury in the eleventh house: Mercury in the eleventh house will seek out like-minded friends and groups. There is a need for intellectual rapport and stimulation. They may have friends of all ages, especially younger. The pursuit of knowledge can be carried out in the company of friends or those who belong to the *group.* Teamwork, especially research and discovery, is indicated.

If there are difficult aspects to Mercury in this house, there may be trouble communicating within the group or expressing to friends. This placement can indicate two or more goals operating at the same time—a curiosity around the nature of collective activities and interest in telepathy and technological forms of communication. Mercury here says *knowledge must be shared.*

Venus in the eleventh house: Venus in the eleventh house can indicate advantage and gain through friendship. If Venus is not in a

challenging aspect, there can be unmitigated support and fulfillment as a direct result of a friend's or group member's actions.
With harsh aspects, the native can make poor choices in friendship
and suffer the consequences.

Here there is a natural talent for uniting people and working in
cooperation with them, especially in the field of visual and performing arts. Usually refined, Venus here can sometimes get entan-
gled with jealousy, overindulgence and rivalry among friends or
between group members. The sign and aspects will indicate how
best to handle these situations. Venus here also places a high value
on the quality of friendships and the integrity of the group. The goddess of love in the eleventh says *camaraderie brings beauty and
success.*

Mars in the eleventh house: Mars in the eleventh house brings
an abundance of energy and fractious enthusiasm to any goals,
groups or organizations it is involved in. There can be conflict between self-will and team spirit. Sometimes this position works best
if the individual can lead the group, organize the event, manage the
assembly. There is a natural affinity for groups of all kinds and, at
the same time, a need for independence and self-direction.

Enthusiasm is infectious, and the native may be able to rally a
gathering into action. This can be important in the field of politics,
rescue missions, explorations and brainstorming. Mars here says
tag! You are it.

Jupiter in the eleventh house: Jupiter in the eleventh house can
attract support and encouragement from friends that help the native
on his or her quest. The intuition is strong and the judgment sound.
With difficult aspects, however, Jupiter here can indicate friends
that sway us from our goals, distracting us with indulgences and
impossible dreams.

This is a future-looking placement, one that keeps the current
goal firmly within sight. There is an ability to multi-task and stay
focused on several projects at once. Groups are important, as are
expanding and varied friendships. Like Mars, Jupiter often wants to
lead the throng. Teaching, education, travel and exploration are
best done in a group or with a friend. Jupiter here says, *the more the
merrier.*

Saturn in the eleventh house: Saturn in the eleventh house makes participation in groups and associations with friends very important and also very troubled at times. These people must learn to work hard to achieve their goals and objectives, asking for help and companionship along the way. The natural tendency is to go it alone; the need is to discover something essential about their affinity with others. Feelings evoked in a group situation can be ones of deep pain and inadequacy. Time, patience and effort are needed to break through this fear of union through participation.

Although experiences in group situations can be fraught with shadow material, Saturn in the eleventh learns more from being with others than being on its own. They can be fantastic organizers, bringing form and structure to a circle of friends or organization. Goals are very important for these people, as is the focus to see them through. They may have friends that are particularly wise or mature. Saturn here says *this island has harbors for many.*

Chiron in the eleventh house: Chiron in the eleventh house can be involved in supervising various kinds of communication services, healing centers and therapy groups. They can be involved in the performing arts, drama or cultural centers, often as a manager or part of the team. There can be a mutual feeling of support from friends, where information and facilitation flows freely both ways. Difficult aspects to Chiron here can indicate challenges in bringing goals to fruition and issues to overcome with friends and group associates. Chiron here says *association with others brings insight.*

Uranus in the eleventh house: Uranus in the eleventh house can indicate change, fluctuation, excitement and upheaval around goals, groups and organizations. They can have a bouquet of friends from all walks of life and divergent lifestyles. There can be a strong feeling of connection with life, and goals can center around manifesting this in a tangible way through telepathy, information technology, astrology, physics, education, and mediation within the group.

Uranus here is happiest when communing with like minds. With difficult aspects, this is not always easy. This placement can get bored easily, requiring large amounts of stimulation. Not every group will measure up to these needs. Goals will change radically over the course of the life. It is important that the native with this position follow every new inspiration, wherever it leads. Uranus here says *let no vision become too fixed.*

Neptune in the eleventh house: Neptune in the eleventh house indicates strong sensitivity to groups, friends and associates. There is a natural feeling of empathy and support toward others who express benevolence for its own sake. Compassion for humankind is powerful with Neptune here and the divine is often sought within the context of the group, large or small.

This placement can spend more time dreaming about goals than reaching them. Strong focus and discipline are essential to achieve tangible results. Depending on the aspects involved, this placement can indicate supportive, endearing friendships or deceptions and betrayals. Friends and groups can also be idealized, or be of a Neptune quality—artistic, romantic, spiritual or dreamy. Neptune here say *communion with all life leads to the divine.*

Pluto in the eleventh house: Pluto in the eleventh house brings the depths of the soul face to face with friends, groups and organizations. Some are better equipped to handle this than others. There is a desire for intensity, provocation and transformation through involvement with others. The native with this position may also be inclined to pick up on the darker and more primordial thoughts and feelings moving through a group. Whatever group they join, it is not likely to be (or remain) lightweight.

Goals need to be set with Pluto in this house, with the realization that they will change and transform, sometimes painfully, from time to time. The native may work with hidden or occult knowledge, psychology, medicine, nuclear physics, politics or issues of power, danger and risk, all within the context of the group or in association with friends. Pluto here says *merging with others for a common purpose brings transformation.*

Twelfth House as an Indicator of Aptitude

The twelfth house traditionally represents our dark and secret hiding places. It is a locale where boundaries blur and forms melt and merge and transfigure. Things are not always what they seem in the twelfth. They are at times confused and painful, yet they also can lead to initiation and understanding.

On a mundane level, this house rules the unconscious mind, the collective unconscious, hospitals and institutions (where people are treated collectively) and charity, given or received. Traditionally, it is said that planets here must serve or suffer.[21] It is a certainty that with any planets in the twelfth house, the native needs to spend some time alone in a sanctuary of his or her making.

The twelfth house also represents a melting down of ego boundaries, a merging with the divine, a loss of specific and personal identity. Not everyone is going to enjoy this experience. Consider the placement of the Sun in Aries in the twelfth in contrast to the Moon in Pisces in the twelfth. Which one is going to feel more at home?

Everything that operates in this house is under the surface, behind the scenes. It represents things that are below our conscious awareness, yet important in terms of how they direct our choices, goals and desires. (Planets here can significantly influence the character of the native's career, mission or profession.) When planets falling in the twelfth house ask, *Where am I?*, the answer is, *I am in my mystique.*

Sun in the twelfth house: The Sun in the twelfth house is a position that needs careful handling. There can be so much psychic sensitivity that the native becomes paranoid and dysfunctional. Here the sense of identity and uniqueness is formed from giving service to others. There has to be a conscious balance between what is for self and what is for the collective. In this position, the balance leans heavily toward delving into the hidden side of the self to provide service for others.

This position can feel a great deal of fulfillment working with others who are in some way limited or afflicted. They may be attracted to the field of medicine (traditional or alternative) certain kinds of therapy (hypnosis, creative visualizations) anesthesiology, occult studies or psychic phenomena. They may be adept musicians or artists. The Sun here says *by merging with the collective, I retrieve who I am.*

Moon in the twelfth house: Moon in the twelfth house is a very sensitive position. The psychic empathy is strong and those with this placement may be open to the feelings and motives of others on an undercurrent level. Sometimes, it may be hard for the person with a twelfth house Moon to distinguish between his or her own feelings and the emotions of those around them.

These people can be very successful in the creative arts by using the non-rational forms of expression to communicate their ideas. Other career paths that take advantage of the intuitive sensitivity to others and the collective include teaching of the young, fiction writing and politics. The Moon here says *dissolve all boundaries with me so we may experience the secrets unknown.*

Mercury in the twelfth house: Mercury in the twelfth house knows how to keep a secret. This placement suggests these natives are not *an open book* when it comes to rational thoughts, ideas and the communication of feelings. This does not mean they are necessarily deceptive; it just means they may at times be hard to fathom.

This placement suggests an attunement to the thoughts buzzing around in the environment. Those with this position need to spend time in self-contemplation and introspection in order to distinguish their own thoughts, goals and ideas from that of the collective. Until they do, they may be easily swayed or manipulated. Aptitudes of this placement include psychic abilities, creative imagination, artistic expression and access to ancient wisdom. Mercury here says *the message lies beneath.*

Venus in the twelfth house: Venus in the twelfth house can indicate a love of and attraction to anything that melts and merges, breaks down boundaries and unites one with the ineffable. This can range from drugs, alcohol and other addictions to sex, art and religious ecstasy. Some of these loves may be beneficial to the native. Others may not.

This position can be associated with a deep compassion for others and works well in the field of medicine, psychology and other therapies. This Venus can also indicate an aptitude for music, fine arts, acting and working behind the scenes (camera, lighting, sound engineers, script writers, directors, producers and artistic agents or managers). Traditionally, Venus here is a hidden guardian angel. The goddess of love in this house says *beauty is found in the hidden things.*

Mars in the twelfth house: Mars in the twelfth house brings its robust energy into a sea of collective feelings. It may take the native a while to get his or her bearings. This Mars can seem mild mannered, but harbors a tremendous amount of energy. It's like a shotgun fired under water. The drive may be toward service or toward domination.

Mars here can be strongly assertive (especially close to the Ascendant) and enjoy talents in sports, athletics, martial arts, debate and adventure in general. It may also disappear, leaving the native with a glum sense of confusion around direction and desires. For Mars to be happy anywhere, it needs to have a goal. Those with this position do best if they put time into defining their goals and desires. Mars here says *hidden aggression contains the greatest power, fair or foul.*

Jupiter in the twelfth house: Jupiter is traditionally at home in the twelfth house and in this house the king of the Olympians expands the already limitless boundaries of the unconscious and imbibes a sense of blessing, optimism and enthusiasm for the future. Here are the talents for work in institutions—hospitals, prisons, schools, universities and other authority bodies. There is a natural flare for success in these fields, as well as in journalism, script writing, acting, executive positions and politics.

Jupiter in the twelfth can bring an aptitude for working behind the scenes, especially in the film industry, in the healing arts or in traditional medicine. These people can working on an organizational level in the area of travel (to hidden, exclusive places), higher education (secret occult teachings or more orthodox schools of thought) or religion. This position always attracts hidden allies along the way. Jupiter here says *I expand the boundaries of the inner unknown.*

Saturn in the twelfth house: Saturn in the twelfth house can manifest as a desire to retreat. This placement can indicate the need for a particularly private life, a protection from the high levels of sensitivity felt in the world. These people can become paranoid if Saturn is afflicted here, or other aspects don't counterbalance the effects. The twelfth house is about dissolving boundaries and entering the unconscious life; Saturn abhors the dissolution, fearing greatly what lurks beneath.

This position requires the facing of great fears of the unknown and uncontrollable, dealing with self-doubt, the feeling of inadequacy, paranoia and guilt. Conversely, once faced honestly and willingly, the issues around Saturn can be put in perspective and the native may benefit from Saturn's strong sense of limits, organizational skills and inner wisdom. The key for these people is to take the world of the unconscious seriously without letting it drown them.

Those with this placement may have talent and ability in the field of science and medicine. They may be mystics, teachers, managers, organizers and those who work with minute and functional details in life (from computer animation to micro-surgery). Saturn here says *as a speaker for the collective unconscious, I find success.*

Chiron in the twelfth house: Chiron in the twelfth house can associate with a particular kind of healing. These people can be found in the mental health field and working as spiritual healers, with dreams and imagination. Even when the methods are unorthodox, they often work through institutions and established organizations. There may be a link between a personal wound and the occupation, making this placement an indication of the *wounded healer*. Chiron here says *I can make the dreams come true.*

Uranus in the twelfth house: Uranus in the twelfth house wants to break down existing structures, although here the structures are so amorphous that they don't know what to push against. There can be frustrations with this position because the native needs to learn how to approach the world of the unconscious in unique and inventive ways. Unhampered, that is exactly what Uranus does.

An aptitude exists for creative approaches in the fields of science, technology, psychology, education and politics. These are the reformers, and once they get their bearings in the sea of the twelfth house, they can intuitively tap into knowledge of a collective nature, using it to enhance and better society. These people need a sanctuary in which to retreat from time to time. They also need to listen to their dreams as blasts of insight and information may come to them in this state. Uranus here says *there are no limitations.*

Neptune in the twelfth house: Neptune is at home in the twelfth house and sometimes this planet gets so comfortable it completely disappears. There can be an inner loneliness, a divine homesickness that can only be appeased by a true connection with the higher self.

Talent resides in the ability to serve others in the fields of science, medicine, physics, or through hospitals and institutions. There can be a strong creative and poetic side that, when unhampered by addiction or substance abuse, can result in success in the fields of fine arts, literature, film and music. Neptune here says *ever seeking; ever deepening.*

Pluto in the twelfth house: Pluto in the twelfth house is highly sensitive to the darker undercurrents in the collective. These people can *feel* silent, repressed and violent trends in the collective and need to protect themselves, possibly by avoiding some types of gatherings. When that is not possible, they may need to get up and leave a group situation when the energy becomes too intense. The point is to listen to the inner warning to avoid becoming a mouthpiece for the darker collective thoughts.

Because Pluto is associated with the collective shadow, those with this placement may find themselves working with it in some way, through crisis situations, counseling, group therapy techniques or law enforcement and crime prevention. They may be involved in the military or deal with darker issues through writing or teaching. They may challenge archaic structures or oppressive governments or institutions. These are the fighters against injustice—Green Peace, Amnesty International, Peace Corps. Pluto is an either/or planet and in the twelfth it is working to transform the collective shadow or adding heap upon heap to it. There is no middle road. Pluto here says *face me you must.*

Part III

Fool or Magician? The Planets and Other Points

To be in a career that correlates with your archetypal make up is a blessing.[22]—Howard Sasportas

*T*he planets are the energy in the chart, the vital forces, the actors whose scripts are read according to their own nature and expertise. Each planet represents an impetus, a strength with a will of its own. Understanding what that will is means being able to live out more of our authentic selves.

Although all the planets seek outer expression and have something valuable to offer, some will have more urgent needs than others. A planet on the Ascendant, for instance, or a planet conjunct the Sun or Moon, may *need* to express itself on a daily basis, bringing its talents and aptitudes with it. Living out those qualities is what makes us feel ourselves—whole, complete and creatively genuine.

The following is a list of the planets and other significant points, describing how they relate to aptitude in the astrological chart. Some points, like the Sun, are of vital importance to everyone because they reflect the striving to become everything we can possibly be. The more we can *do* our Sun sign, for instance, the more fulfilled we feel.

Saturn also takes on crucial importance because it often represents what we are desperately afraid of facing, as well as what we are destined to live out to the fullest. Expressing Saturn may be an arduous journey, although that achievement is its own reward. When Saturn is honored, we can find ourselves living in his golden age of enlightenment.

Again, each planet has its own treasures to offer in terms of talent and ability; discovering them is the key to success. Consider the following delineations when reading the horoscope in terms of what may be augmented and animated in the native.

Sun as a Sign of Capability: What We Are Becoming

"The sun reflects the urge within every human being to express himself, and grow into what he potentially is."[23]—Liz Greene

The Sun, natural ruler of Leo, is a potent indicator of the individual's authentic essence. Its house position and sign suggest a basic sense of purpose, fulfillment and actualization in life. However, the Sun does not represent a *given*. We don't automatically have all the solar traits indicated by our Sun sign. It is much more an assignment than a published thesis, and we have to work hard for most or all of our lives to complete it.

Just because one has the Sun in Aries doesn't mean he or she is ardent and assertive. However, being ardent and assertive can help that individual become more of who she or he is. Having Sun in Virgo doesn't automatically make one organized and discerning, although being those things can bring that person in touch with his or her native self.

Understanding our solar needs can go a long way toward developing natural abilities. If someone with the Sun in Gemini lives in isolation and can not communicate easily, he or she will not feel completely accomplished. If someone with the Sun in Scorpio has nothing in which to become intensely involved, he or she will not feel successful, no matter what the bank book or public reviews say. We need to *do* our Sun to feel like the person we're meant to be. This solar drive for significance is exemplified in Apollo, the Greek god of light.

Apollo was the son of Zeus and Leto and the twin brother of Artemis, virgin goddess of the hunt. He was called the dazzling *lord of light,* the solar deity. His origins are confused, his personalities multiple. He is the god of light yet not the Sun itself. He is the god of creativity and leader of the Muses.

Apollo discovered not only the bow and arrow, but also the lyre. He was the god of sudden death as well as healing. Music, marksmanship and, later, divination were his domain. He never shunned battle or the chance to compete for domination and killed many a foe, yet he also was a shepherd god, guardian of the vulnerable flock and herd.

Apollo was most honored and respected by visiting his oracle. This implies that if we ask the right questions, if we take the time to look within at our own inner workings, we will be blessed with guidance. It is important to note here that the guidance offered by Apollo's oracle was not always easy to understand or execute. Asking the question though, seems paramount.

Apollo also has a lot to do with individual creativity and the forces that guide it. Hesiod said: *"For it is through the Muses and far shooting Apollo that there are singers and harpers upon the earth."*[24]

The sign and position of the Sun can point strongly to one's calling and aptitude and the area of life the individual most needs to cultivate. The vocations, careers and activities associated with the Sun's placement are varied and can be acted out on different levels. For instance, Sun in Aries may have the aptitude to become a firefighter, blacksmith, metallurgical engineer, glass cutter, surgeon, welder or hairdresser. These activities all fit under the Aries occupational umbrella. Remember too that there can be movement between the different areas of expression as in when someone majors in engineering only to go on and study medicine, or works as a hair stylist and later becomes a horseshoer. The important thing is to live out the archetype and be the people we are meant to be.

Moon as a Sign of Higher Instinct: What Comes Naturally

However safe the way may be, nothing can be done without the benefit of Luna.[25]*—Marsilio Facino*

For many people, the Moon constitutes what comes naturally, what feels like love in terms of nurturing and what feels like comfort and familiarity. If the Moon is not aspected by rigorous outer planet contacts, it is likely to function as a magnet, bringing to material form the needs of the body and personality. Following a course in life that honors the Moon will add to a personal sense of inner fulfillment. If, however, the Moon is not happy in a particular job, project or activity, it may become the saboteur in covert and surreptitious ways.

The Moon rules the feeling sign Cancer. It will express in individual ways through the natal sign, house and aspect placement. By looking to the Moon, we can discover ways and means of encouraging self-nourishing and following an innate and natural path. Some astrologers believe that the Moon sign, along with the South Lunar Node, is an indication of what was mastered or attempted in a past life.

Whether the Moon is indicative of previous experience, it certainly exemplifies what is familiar and natural, although not always comfortable to the other planets in the chart. How the Moon relates to the Sun by aspect, for instance, is a good indication of how these two archetypes intermesh. A Pisces Moon may have a natural tendency to blend in with those around it. This might clash if the individual also has the Sun in Leo and strives for distinction within the group. A Libra Moon may want to express loveliness and beauty, although that could mean conflict if the individual also has the Sun in Aries (Full Moon) and is forever stirring things up. Yet when the Sun and Moon are in conjunction (New Moon in the same sign) or in other harmonious aspects, there can be a compatibility of intention, talent and aptitude. The drive for distinction blends nicely with a sense of the natural. The archetypes are aligned, the lunar goddess is well pleased.

Representations of the Moon goddesses come in varied forms in mythology, from Artemis the maiden, free and wild, to Hera the matron, adult wife, mother and co-ruler of Mt. Olympus, to the dark Moon goddesses like Hecate and Ereshkagal, who represent the domain of the witch, the crone, the black virgin.[26] All these figures represent an aspect of the feminine, the cycle of life and death and the manifestation of form in the world.

These figures also represent something instinctual, something innate that must not be abandoned nor allowed to overtake and devour. Balancing the needs of the Moon with the rest of the chart is a key to healthy development, emotionally and physically. What Luna represents may come easily or it may come hard, but it must not be ignored because it is part of our nature, part of our path to becoming who we are meant to be.

Mercury as a Sign of Choices: What We Think and Say

Through him (Mercury) we become conscious by remembering ourselves, our origins and our reason for being.[27] *—Ean Begg*

Mercury is the winged messenger of the gods. It represents communication in all its various forms: the written and spoken word, talking, teaching, lecturing, learning and all kinds of commerce, above and below the board. It is about travel from point to point, traversing the familiar roads, following the god down the appointed path. Mercury is fleet, ever changing and anxious to be on to the next task. If Mercury has to sit still, it may fidget and get bored, and a bored Mercury is trouble on wheels.

This is when Mercury transforms into the trickster. In this guise, it may misinform, lead astray. It might point to the wrong fork in the road, steal our ideas away in the night and leave us dumbfounded. It is completely unabashed in this role, amoral, without guilt or remorse. It stands to reason, then, that the *misunderstandings* caused by this trickster archetype are not necessarily to our detriment—what seems foul may actually be fair, guiding us to a new horizon. Winged Mercury certainly can create change and get us moving, regardless of the direction.

Mercury rules two signs: knowledge hungry Gemini and analytical Virgo. It is the god of choice, standing at the crossroads, helping us to decide which way to go next, which path to take in the myriad course of life. Alciato's *Book of Emblems* describes it like this: *At the crossroads is a mountain of stones; the shortened figure of a god rises above it, figured as far down as his chest. This then is the hill of Mercury. Traveler, raise up garlands to the god, that to you he may show the proper road.*[28]

There is in this description the intimation that to some, at least, Mercury may show the improper road. With this god, there is always risk.

Mercury is important in terms of aptitude because it represents how we learn, think and communicate. Mercury's sign and house placement and aspects all flavor the conscious mind: *what we think and what we think we think.* Because it is so close to the Sun, Mercury will always be found in the sign before, the sign after or the same sign as the Sun. When it is in the same sign, expressing Mercury will feel especially meaningful because the two planets represent the same orientation. When the sign is different from the Sun, it may feel difficult to express our true selves openly, or there could be conflict between what we say and what we feel is true. Particular effort needs to be placed on both archetypes when the Sun and Mercury are in different signs.

Honoring Mercury gives us a feeling of dynamic self-expression. When in touch with this god, we are in touch with our authentic beliefs, ideas and goals. The original purpose of astrology was to discern the ambiguous intentions of the gods, and what better way than to heed their messenger, winged Mercury.

Venus as a Sign of Desire: What We Love to Attract

It is no longer a heat concealed in my blood, it is Venus herself grasping her pray.—Jean Baptiste Racine

Venus symbolizes attraction, desire, longing, luxury and bliss. She is rapacious, artistic, heady in her loveliness, jealous and protective of her sense of values. Understanding Venus means knowing what we love and value and allowing it to come to us. This is the planet of pleasure and social interaction, although what brings pleasure varies from person to person.

Venus portrays our talents by describing what we naturally find worthy of pursuit and development. It may represent the way we go about nurturing our goals and how we value our achievements, fact or fantasy. Where Venus is by sign and house can lead to where we gain support from inner talents and abilities to outer recognition and aid.

94

Venus/Aphrodite was the goddess of love, mother of Eros, wife to Mars/Hephaistos and lover of many, gods and mortals alike. She personifies sensuality, beauty and allure. She is the goddess of relationship, body, sex, pleasure and imagination. Marsilio Ficino, masterful Florentine astrologer, felt that Venus was closely aligned with *spirit: "Venus's gift, then, is spirit, but it is a peculiar kind of spirituality, one quite sensual. There is spirit to be gained from her sensuality, sexuality and absorption in pleasure, and therefore her domain is good for the soul.*[29]

Honoring Venus can lead us to a greater clarity around what we desire and what we will find pleasure in pursuing. The passion of Venus can inflame the heart and drive us to express our talents buried deeply within.

Part of this honoring includes the indulgence of imagination, the fantasies and daydreams that allow us to project what we long to become. Believing is the first step in creation and to imagine is to begin to believe. In this case, the luxury of fantasy may lead us to our calling, show us the way to go. Those unwilling to imagine are perhaps unwilling also to bring a piece of their creative spirit to life.

Venus rules two signs: earthy, temporal Taurus and social, cultured Libra. The former is more interested in tangible outcomes, sensual pleasure and all forms of mundane security, including money and possessions. The latter is more concerned with artistic pleasure, social refinement and cultural interaction. Both get what they want through the receptive power of attraction—a pull, as it were, not a push.

To pay homage to Venus is to awaken our powers of attraction, love, beauty and sensual pleasure. By allowing Venus room in our lives, we can be sure that the talents and aptitudes that we pursue are in alignment with what we innately value and appreciate. Balancing Venus' needs with our solar, lunar and Mercurial ones, means we can truly do what we value and love.

Mars as a Sign of Energy:
Where Our Power Lies

I conceived the libido as a psychic analogue of physical energy...I no longer wished to speak of the instincts of hun-

ger, aggression, and sex but to regard all these phenomena as expressions of psychic energy.[30]—C. G. Jung

Mars is the energy that gets us out of bed in the morning. It pushes us forward into life with the drive to fulfill basic instinctual needs such as food, water, shelter and sex. In modern terms, this may translate into seeking a job, searching for the right house or apartment, taking courses of study to further our goals and mixing in social activities to meet a potential partner. A functioning Mars also keeps us from being abused.

Mars has much to do with a healthy aggression—the force within that helps us get our way, stand up for our rights and become self-directing. Mars has been easier for men to access because society found the self-actualized male more acceptable than the independent female. This is in the process of transformation, and the results are that more women identify with their own Mars as opposed to projecting it onto the father, husband or son. Without a healthy, active Mars, male or female, we run the risk of becoming doormats.

Mars is necessary to keep us from being pushed around. It is the power that helps us stand up on our own two feet and get what we want, say what we feel, actualize our will. If we disassociate from our Mars, we become weak. Other people tell us what to do, where to be and how to act. No Mars equates with no libido, no healthy aggression, no self-direction and no willpower.

Too much Mars, however, makes us arrogant, overbearing and contemptuous. We push others around, demand they bend to our will and ignore their rights. We become the officious intermeddler, the tyrannical boss, the oppressive or even cruel spouse. Too much Mars means we are a walking stick of domination, ready to crack down on everything and anything. Clearly, a healthy balanced Mars is preferable to the over or under expressed one. Often it is a case of fine adjustments, learned and developed through life.

Mars was the god of war, a bundle of raw fiery energy that cut a wide swath. He was sometimes brutal in his expression of power. Although extremely competitive, he didn't always win. Yet he always rose to the challenge. In terms of aptitude and talents, an activated Mars is essential for providing the energy and drive to achieve our goals and become who we are meant to be.

Where Mars is in the chart by sign, house and aspect indicates how best to express our will in life and how to go about getting what we want. Strong placements of Mars can indicate an aptitude for Mars talents: competitive sports, physical and athletic challenges, positions of command, including the military, or other occupations that require risk, bravery, danger, assertive power and leadership. Mars is not a natural team player unless it leads the pack.

Mars rules two signs in the zodiac, Aries and Scorpio. Both of these reflect a certain push and assertion: Aries is the adventurous assertion of the will and Scorpio the intense assertive drive to create. Honoring Mars in our lives is vital to fulfillment of our talents, dreams and aptitude. Without it, we won't be bothered to find out who we really are.

Jupiter as a Sign of Meaning:
What Gives Us Purpose

And this song is considered a perfect gem, And as to the meaning, it's what you please.—C. S. Calverley

Isabel Hickey[31] said that Jupiter holds the secret to living life fully. Ruling the superconscious self, it represents that part of us that has no limitations, no restrictions or confinement. It is the principle of expansion and is associated with optimism, self-confidence and enthusiasm. Jupiter, king of the gods on Mt. Olympus, rules our innate drive to seek meaning and purpose in life. It is this sense of meaning, if we have it, that contributes to the joy and fullness inherent in Jupiter.

The adage, *lack of enthusiasm is the sign of a wrong goal,* could easily be translated into: *the lack of Jupiter is the sign of a wrong goal.* We need our Jupiter, our sense of meaning and purpose, to feel like we are on the correct path. When Jupiter is happy, energy flows; no matter what the prevailing circumstances are, we feel a sense of rightness about our endeavors. Jupiter is not necessarily a guarantee of success in the conventional sense, but it is a guarantee of inner fulfillment while we pursue our goals.

As an indicator or aptitude, a strong Jupiter equates with promotions, expansiveness, popularity, success and generosity. Too much Jupiter can lead to overconfidence, conceit and indulgence, to the detriment of self and others. Too little and there seems to be no point. This planet represents our ability to do things and become what we want because we believe we can. The preservation of these beliefs is also the realm of Jupiter.

Jupiter, ruler of both far seeking Sagittarius and mystical Pisces, preserves through ritual and ceremony by marking the rights of passage in our lives. Regardless of the belief system, from Pagan to Christian, Judaism to Hindu, Occult to Bahai, the feeling of meaning and purpose is evoked just the same, and that is a very important process in life.

It is said that we must never marry outside of our religion, and although this is a debatable topic, it stems from the belief that for a successful union, we must have our Jupiters aligned. This holds true also for the pursuit and development of our talents and aptitudes.

Where Jupiter is by sign, house and aspect tells us what we must integrate into our lives to feel whole and ready to step forward with a sense of meaning and personal truth. Without Jupiter, we go forth without the belief that we can succeed, if we go forth at all.

Saturn as a Sign of Challenge: What Is Vital to Achieve

A man who fears suffering is already suffering from what he fears.—Michael D. Montaigne

Saturn is a challenge, no way around it. He is the god of boundaries, the ring past naught, the guardian at the gate. Most of us will not begin to come to terms with this archetype and face the tasks required by the lord of the Titans until after the first return at about age twenty-nine. In the meantime, we are more likely to project Saturn outward as a series of blocks, controls, authority figures and essential failures, real or imagined. It is no wonder Saturn evokes so much fear and loathing (and misunderstanding) in the hearts of many.

Initially, Saturn's placement in the chart represents a set of true talents, aptitudes and abilities that seem completely and painfully out of reach. They may be so foreign to us that we can't even imagine them as valid goals. The very thought may even repulse us, engendering a strong negative emotional reaction.

As we mature, we start to recognize that other people achieve these things, (our inner talents) and we may begin to dream of them ourselves. We may have friends that do them, or admire specialists in those fields. We may even marry someone who is pursuing or achieving this seemingly ineffable goal. Then, at some point, if we are fortunate, we face the beast and realize that it is actually our goal, our dream and our fancy to pursue this hard objective of desire. At this point we gain a little bit bigger piece of ourselves and become that much more complete.

Saturn feels, at first, like a wound that we want no one to see or touch. After all, he was the King of the Titans who devoured all his creations the minute they were born because he thought they would usurp him. Not a lot of confidence there. Not a lot of room for blossoming creativity either.

Where Saturn is in the chart by sign, house and planetary aspect is where we have great apprehension. We meet our shadow, the dark and undifferentiated side of the unconscious that evokes disgust. It evokes dread. It can define our limitations so acutely that we feel paralyzed. When Saturn whispers hello, we want to run away as fast as our little legs can take us.

Where Saturn is in the chart is also where we have our greatest potential to achieve fulfillment. It is of such great importance that we may never feel our life was fully lived if we can not at least pursue it. This placement, through hard work and painstaking effort, is where we can become proficient, acknowledged and successful. It is the pot of gold at the end of the rainbow, but the rainbow looks and feels like a demon's lair, dark, damp, forbidding.

Saturn rules both the ambitious Capricorn and the evocative Aquarius, and facing this planet may be a large portion of our life's task. It is certainly an indicator of talent and potential, although it will not blossom on its own or without great and sustained effort. Saturn requires that we put in the hours and face the keeper at each gate. Not everyone is willing to meet such a challenge, although they may miss out on their life's calling if they bypass this god.

Saturn is somewhat of a realist, a scientist and an architect. When placed close to the angles or conjunct or opposition a personal planet, we may be more inclined to pursue qualities that reflect the taskmaster: teaching, biology, science, chemistry, building, crystals, orthopedics, dermatology and research into things of the past (occult/archeology).

Chiron as a Sign of Inspiration: What Is the Key?

The value of compassion cannot be over-emphasized. Anyone can criticize. It takes a true believer to be compassionate. No greater burden can be borne by an individual than to know no one cares or understands.— Arthur H. Stainback

Chiron is the wounded healer. He bore the pain of isolation, rejection, ridicule and mortal wounding, yet still he healed others. He is a hero in the greatest sense of the word as the ancient Greeks intended: *heroes: to protect, to preserve, to reserve.*

Where Chiron is in the natal chart is where we feel a wound that can allow us to empathize with others, to build, show and share our compassion. He is the archetype of the activist in all helping professions. He also was good at strategy and the art of war, thus resulting in his association with the martial arts. He trained the children of kings and gods to become heroes, instilling in them the audacity to attempt. In this vein, Chiron spurs us on to do the impossible.

When Chiron is significantly placed (on the angles, conjunct the Sun, Moon or personal planets, conjunct the North Node) talents and occupations representing Chiron's nature may be pursued. These include all forms of counseling and psychotherapy, paramedical fields, chiropractic, herbal medicine, homeopathy and various Eastern disciplines such as meditation, martial arts and acupuncture.

Where Chiron is in the natal chart and where it touches by transit is where we must learn the depths of compassion and humanitarian proclivity. If we ignore this step, our wound will always bleed. Honor it and Chiron is the key to new levels of understanding.

Natal Chiron in Aries/first house: Particularly extreme in action, the adventure and challenge outweighs the destination. Chiron here prepares the hero for life as a series of challenges, leading to greater and greater goals, risks and results. Ways and means involve energy, freedom, physical development (sports), independence and leadership. Consider Tyler Hamilton, the international cyclist with Chiron in Aries in the tenth house, who finished fourth in the 2003 Tour de France with a fractured clavicle! Carl Jung, with Chiron in Aries in the second house, pioneered into the depths of psychology, fathering "Jungian Analysis" and Louis Pasteur, with Chiron in Aries in the sixth, made breakthrough discoveries in immunology and microbiology.

Natal Chiron in Taurus/second house: Pushing boundaries beyond their limits, Chiron here has tangible and practical results in mind. The Centaur goads individuals through the senses—taste, touch, smell, hearing, seeing. The physical realm and the body become the challenge! Elizabeth Kubler-Ross, with Chiron in Taurus in the second, pushed through the conventional attitudes towards death and dieing, creating new horizon of understanding and empathy for many. Helen Keller, deaf and blind author and lecturer, surpassed extreme limitations in the realm of the senses to achieve the seemingly impossible.

Natal Chiron in Gemini/third house: Here the Centaur seeks the far reaches of the imagination through ideas, thoughts and communications of all kinds. The goal is intellectual, conceptual—ever expanding the boarders of the immediate environment. Author and humorist Mark Twain, with Chiron in Gemini in the seventh house and the mathematician/philosopher Sir Isaac Newton, with Chiron in Gemini in the eighth house both goaded their contemporaries with provocative thinking, writing and publishing.

Natal Chiron in Cancer/fourth house: Here is the placement astrologer Dale O'Brien suggests the suffering Wounded Healer archetype would probably be most applicable. The sensitivity, coupled with the need to be needed, may result in the empathic healer/counselor/creative artist, and sometimes the heartbreaking victim. A tragic example includes Vaslac Nijinsky, extraordinary ballet dancer who died in an asylum. Also, Tchaikovsky, Nostradamus, and T.E. Lawrence—men who suffered deep emotional turmoil in the processes of their creative and visionary lives. More up beat representations of Chiron in Cancer are Claude Monet, stretching artistic boundaries and founding impressionism and Voltaire, author, skeptic and philosopher known for his "cheek."

Natal Chiron in Leo/fifth house: Here Chiron really wants to play! Risk and daring tumble and plunge the native into creative adventures, romance, art, drama, literature and speculation. The propelling force is distinction and individuality. Harrison Ford, with Chiron in Leo conjunct Mars in the tenth, lives out a rapacious, cheeky and indomitable character through Indian Jones, Han Solo, and the more mature special agent... Author Henry Miller, Chiron in Leo in the fifth, provoked obscenity trials in the USA with his "Tropic" books and Fannie Brice (Ziegfeld Folly's) and Barbara Streisand, both with Chiron in Leo, were venerated for their "Funny Girl" comedienne performances.

Natal Chiron in Virgo/sixth house: Chiron in the sign of the Vestal Virgin can teach the audacity to attempt through devotion, focus, endurance and autonomy. There is a self-containment here, and a fine skilled development of techniques, that can achieve outstanding results. Painter of the Sistine Chappell, Michelangelo's Chiron in Virgo in the ninth broke tradition, and the patients of those around him, to create one of the world's most famous works of art. Star Wars creator George Lucas, with his Chiron in Virgo on the cusp of the fifth, continues to take cinematic techniques to their extreme with his visionary trilogies. Classical guitarist Andreas Segovia and spiritual leader yogi Paramahansa Yogananda both with Chiron in Virgo took traditional techniques to master levels.

Natal Chiron in Libra/seventh house: The impetus and voracity of Chiron here lives through the realm of artistic expression, mental reflection and the mysteries of socially significant relating. Libra, the iron fist inside the velvet glove, wants to make things fair but firm, elegant yet rational. Chiron takes it to an extreme. Both Martin Luther and Judda Krishnamurti, with Chiron in Libra in the eighth, rebelled against the constraints of their religious orders. Krishnamurti went on to preach salvation by "right conduct" and Luther founded the protestant church. Rudolf Valentino, with Chiron in Libra in the seventh, brought the arts of romantic love and intimacy to the silver screen. Mary Shelly, with Chiron in Libra wrote Frankenstein, a vivid exploration of the relationship between beauty and beast, man and god.

Natal Chiron in Scorpio/eighth house: Chiron's penchant for

102

impudence merges with the erotic here, making taboo adventures of all kinds appealing. Amelia Earhart, first female pilot to cross the Atlantic Ocean, had Chiron in Scorpio opposite Asc. She not only dared the limits of her profession, breaking more world records than any other woman pilot, she also did much to pave the way for other women during a time when wearing pants, let alone flying stunt planes, was somewhat taboo for females. Frank Abagnale Jr., notorious con-artist, forger and impersonator, pushed the limits by manipulating other people's money into his own pockets. His taboo ventures eluded the authorities for years, while he was still in his teens! Alexander Pushkin, poet/novelist with Chiron in Scorpio conjunct Neptune, was killed in a duel! Notice the flare for the dramatic!

Natal Chiron in Sagittarius/ninth house: Chiron's push can be particularly bombastic in this fiery sign of the Centaur. The goad to expand boundaries to the extreme, blast through limits and explore the unknown can spin the native off into wild and risky adventures. John Milton, author of the epic Paradise Lost, lived his heroic adventure through literature, as did Robert Louis Stenvenson—Dr. Jeckle and Mr. Hyde, Treasure Island, etc. Alfred Hitchcock, with Chiron conjunct Uranus in Sagittarius, explored the terrain of mystery and horror through his groundbreaking films. Eugene Ormandy, Hungarian born prodigy, traveled to the USA with less than a nickel and went on to conduct the Philadelphia Orchestra for an unprecedented 44 years. It was the first American symphony to perform in the People's Republic of China!

Natal Chiron in Capricorn/tenth house: Here Chiron lives within the serious and sometimes stern boundaries of Saturn. Goals must be practical, of social significance and ambitious. Results matter. Success matters! Nazim Hikmet, Turkish poet, revolutionary and political prisoner with Chiron in Capricorn, pushed political boundaries, endured restraint, limitations and exile, all while producing some of the last century's most simple, profound and moving poetry. George Orwell, with Chiron in Capricorn in the fourth, explored comparable limitations and human atrocities in his literary masterpiece, 1984. Three other writers with Chiron in Capricorn labored for years on single works—Samuel Johnson, who compiled the first dictionary, Noah Webster who worked 20 years on his dictionary, and Christopher Isherwood who translated the entire Bagavad-gita.

Natal Chiron in Aquarius/eleventh house: Here Chiron prods towards even larger goals, not unlike the task of Prometheus steeling fire from the gods. To become everything we can possibly be, and bring the rest of humanity along with us, is not too small a sight for the Centaur in this position. Thinking outside of the traditional box—way outside—is the nature of this placement. Rudolf Steiner, philosopher and teacher with Chiron in Aquarius in the ninth house promoted anthroposophy (mankind as center of perceptions). Francesco Petrarch, renaissance founder of Humanism, renewed cultural and artistic interest, instilling a fresh belief in man and his capabilities. His Chiron was also in Aquarius as was Sigmund Freud's, whose third house placement pushed the boundaries of the human mind.

Natal Chiron in Pisces/twelfth house: When Chiron is found in the sign of Pisces, it is through dreams, healing, music, medicine, oceanic exploration, poetry and the longing for a return to the spirit that captivates and compels. The farthest reaches of the imagination become the Centaur's playground. Hedy Lamarr, Chiron in Pisces in the tenth house, first actress to perform in the nude and inventor of a missile tracking system based on her understanding of musical harmonics, pushed boundaries in not only film and music but the ministry of defense! Jacques Cousteau, famous oceanographer with Chiron in Pisces, explored the unknown depths of the sea, revealing his discoveries to the rest of the world. Another link to the sea is Arthur Miller, writing the heroic adventures of his Chiron in Pisces into Moby Dick. Working in hospitals, Jonas Salk with Chiron in Pisces, was the first to develop a successful vaccine against Polio.

Uranus as a Sign of Uniqueness: What Do We Dare?

Life without liberty is like a body without spirit.—Kahlil Gibran, *The Vision*

Uranus takes about seven years to travel through each sign and where it is by house in the natal chart will be more personal than where it is by sign. The sign will associate with a mini-generation of individuals born close to the same decade. In terms of Uranus as an indicator of aptitude and talent, it represents a powerful god, one to be respected.

Uranus, new ruler of Aquarius, is about freedom, autonomy, self-will and individuality. If it is in a prominent position in the chart, these qualities must be respected. This is not the planet of the follower, the pushover or the *yes* man/woman. It is not about long-term stability at the price of growth. It is not about keeping things quiet. Uranus is about change and it doesn't mind the turmoil of disruption it can take to make that happen.

People who are *Uranian* need to instigate change, alter the status quo, drive the message home, take the political stand and express their unique and sometimes unorthodox views. They can get a little weird. They are prone to rebel, shock, trick and surprise. If they do not do these things, then shock, rebellion and surprise *happens* to them. They may think it is the world playing havoc with their lives, although it is really their own selves pulling the rug out from under their feet. Anything to get out of a rut.

Consciously honoring this god of change is vital if the individual with a strong Uranus is to feel happy and fulfilled. Ignored, the god of the starry heavens will rain down an array of unexpected and severing events that can make the most subdued life seem like a carnival—from the outside. On the inside it may feel completely out of control. Best let a bit of the bizarre into the life as a matter of course, lest the road becomes too predictable and mundane. Banality is sure to catch this god's eye!

Neptune as a Sign of the Ineffable: Where We Seek the Divine

You are not wrong who deem
That my days have been a dream;
Yet if hope has flown away
In a night, or in a day,
In a vision, or in none,
Is it therefore the less gone?
All that we see or seem
Is but a dream within a dream—Edgar Allan Poe

Neptune, new ruler of Pisces, moves even more slowly than Uranus through the signs, spending about fifteen years, sometimes more and sometimes less, in each. Many of us around the same age share the sign of Neptune, though the house placement will be unique, as will the transits to the personal planets.

Neptune creates a theme, an aura of energy, in each sign that we are often not conscious of, yet it always has something to do with a longing for the divine. In Libra, it is the longing for the good, true and beautiful relationship. In Scorpio, it is the longing for intense transformation through meditation, magic, drugs or psychological therapies. In Sagittarius, it is the longing for expansion of boundaries of the mind, body and spirit, the uncovering of the veils.

Wherever Neptune is by sign, house and aspect is where we seek redemption, where we want to go for solace with the god. It also says something about our aptitudes and abilities, especially if connected to the personal planets or angles in the natal chart.

When Neptune floats dreamlike near the Sun, Moon or Ascendant, we imbibe some of the essence, we become *Neptunian*. The boundaries waver, the walls that divide the realms dissolve and we become sensitive to energy, feelings, moods and realities that may otherwise go unnoticed. We become a psychic sponge.

This can translate into a talent in the field of medicine, healing, counseling and other helping professions. It can also make us so sensitive that we can not cope easily with other people's pain. It may come out in a flare for the imaginable realm, as expressed in forms of art, theater, dance, creative writing, fashion design and animation. Anything that allows us to dip into the dark sea of the collective unconscious, bring up a treasure and then display it for others, fits the Neptune archetype. Those at the cutting edge of their field set trends, make headlines and often become famous. They may also fall into that sea of collective soup, drowning in the alcohol, designer drugs, megalomania and temporary madness that Neptune can also usher in.

A dance with Neptune is a mixed blessing, as are contacts with all the outer planets. The potential for success and fulfillment rides the double-edged sword of mania, yet the longing can not be denied. To hide from the fate of Neptune is as foolish as hiding from our own true self.

Pluto as a Sign of Transformation: What We Don't Understand

Far or forgot to me is near;
Shadow and sunlight are the same;
The vanished gods to me appear;
And one to me are shame and fame.
They reckon ill who leave me out;
When me they fly, I am the wings;
I am the doubter and the doubt,
And I the hymn the Brahmin sings.
—Ralph Waldo Emerson

Pluto, new ruler of Scorpio, is the outermost planet in our known solar system. It takes an average of twenty years to pass through a sign, although Scorpio will see it pass in less than fifteen years and Taurus will host it for closer to thirty. The orbit is quite eccentric.

Pluto is the god of death, a relentless image of transformation. It shrouds itself in mystery, making it very difficult to understand the needs and drives of this archetype. Much of what Pluto has to say is said to the unconscious. Like the other outer planets before it, its nature is difficult to grasp with the conscious mind.

This does not mean Pluto is weak. Pluto's power is irrevocable and associated with what has been written, what is our fate. Even the king of the gods must bow to the lord of the underworld, and that unquestionably is the realm of Pluto—the dark and mysterious labyrinth of the unconscious mind.

Honoring Pluto, then, can be tricky. (If we are not conscious of our deep and inner needs, we will ignore them.) Part of Pluto is the inner journey into the depths of the soul to discover those needs, to understand ourselves, to become more self-aware. It is easy to see how Pluto is related to forms of psychotherapy, occult practices, research of all kinds, and the propensity to live on *the edge.*

A strong Pluto in the chart will thrive on danger, risk, life and death. The more we have to lose, the greater the peril, the more we are aware of the nature of life itself. We know what it is we may be about to lose.

Aptitudes related to Pluto shine in the fields of search and rescue, emergency medicine and all situations involving life and death: law enforcement, crisis counseling, rehabilitation centers, extreme sports.

Pluto surfaces in the fields of the occult and of psychology, where we walk the line between unconscious and conscious, madness and sanity. It is also an appropriate archetype for the politician because they are in touch with mass consciousness. Crowd surfing in a mosh pit ten thousand strong with Pennywise raging on stage is also a Plutonian experience. There are many ways, fortunately, to meet the god. Something for everyone.

If Pluto is intimately combined with the personal planets or angles of the natal chart, then meet it we must. The only choice involved is how.

South Node: What Used to Work

They spend their time mostly looking forward to the past.— John Osborne

The South Node is a hypothetical point where the Moon descends the ecliptic (the imaginary path of the sun around the earth). The psychological interpretation has to do with patterns that are familiar and comfortable—even in the *devil you know* sense of the word. The more occult meaning has to do with past lives, people and experiences that shape our present life.

The South Node always shows the way of least resistance; the habit patterns of other lives that should be outgrown or discarded.[32]

Either interpretation focuses on the unconscious nature of the South Node. It is a pull-back into the well-versed and customary way of doing, being and responding. This may be something we need to move beyond; it may also at times be a source of security, nourishment and solace. It may be a place to rest, to take time out, even for just a little while. To get caught there, however, is seemingly counter productive.

Understanding the South Node's orientation by sign and house position can help us see what may be *easy*. It may also show us where we become trapped, lazy or stagnant. The general movement needs to be away from the South Node and toward the North.

North Node:
What We Need to Develop

Trust no future, howe're pleasant
Let the dead past bury its dead
Act,—act in the living present
Heart within, and God overhead.—H. W.
Longfellow

The North Node is always opposite the South Node by sign and house. It is a symbol of where we need to put our energy, where we can strive to become more proficient, more accustomed, more secure. It may not be a natural feeling; it may only be embraced with great effort over years.

If we have the South Node in Cancer, the North Node will be in Capricorn, and our South Node familiarity will be around security and co-dependency. We may want to rely heavily on family for our sense of self. Put it in the eleventh house and we can be easily absorbed by the group or collective. The North Node in Capricorn says we must learn to stand on our own two feet. We must gain a level of self-sufficiency to become everything we are meant to be. In the fifth house, we must do this through the development of our own creative self-expression.

The North Node by sign and house placement always shows the path, although there may be plenty of resistance. The following is a brief guide to the pull of the Nodes. Please note that the qualities in the South Node sign are not *bad;* they simply have been developed, or overdeveloped, and need the balance of the opposing sign. The more time we spend contemplating our own nodal positions and what they represent, the more detailed the delineation becomes.

North Node in Aries, South Node in Libra: The North Node in Aries suggests the need to embrace the archetype of the Ram. With this placement, we need to seek, explore, assert and insist. We need to learn how to be the boss and get our own way. At the risk of being bombastic and egotistical, we need to explore our own self and the power we can wield.

The South Node in Libra suggests that in the past we were adjusting, harmonizing and willing to be all things to all people. This may be a comfortable state in which we sometimes want to hide.

The pull of the North Node encourages us away from this *keep everything nice on the surface* approach into the world of self-will.

North Node in Taurus, South Node in Scorpio: With the North Node in Taurus, the need is to embrace the tangible, practical and sometimes sensual aspects of life. We need to find out what we value materialistically, emotionally and spiritually. This placement also benefits from seeking out the little pleasures in life!

The South Node in Scorpio may have a habit of merging energy with others, being a support to them, physically or psychologically. This offering of *the crutch* could keep others from finding their own strength. There may also be a past sense of obsession with other people or things. It may be easier to get *intense* than to get to *work*.

North Node in Gemini, South Node in Sagittarius: The North Node in Gemini suggests the need to develop the intellect, communication skills, adaptability and above all, the sense of trickery and fun. An optimistic outlook and the gregarious embracing of relatives can help launch this Node on the right path.

With the pull of Sagittarius coming from the South Node, we may find our energy goes out everywhere without a point of focus. Much can be spilled and wasted. We may hide behind sweeping concepts and beliefs that have no basis in verified wisdom. We may be too easily swayed; too gullible. The pull of the North Node says, *do your own research.* Let the knowledge you discover now govern your actions.

North Node in Cancer, South Node in Capricorn: With the North Node here, we may need to learn how to live symbiotically. There is an urge to develop a sense of family, nurturing, sensitivity and compassion toward those we love. There are many kinds of family, not all of them blood ties. This position, above all, says to build one.

The South Node in Capricorn suggests that, in the past, the emphasis was based on self-sufficiency, independent capability and generalized empire building. There may be a cool detachment toward others and an abhorrence to asking for help. It may have been right to develop this autonomy in the past, although the pull of the North Node says it is time to learn how to need and be needed.

North Node in Leo, South Node in Aquarius: With the North

110

Node here, the need is to develop a deep sense of creative self-expression and the joy and self-respect that comes with it. Individuation becomes vital. No longer is it appropriate to go with the group. North Node in Leo says we must develop our own unique selves and proudly take the honor that comes with it.

South Node in Aquarius suggests that, in the past, we have gained our sense of identity from the group, from our ideals, nationality or beliefs. We gained strength from being part of a strong assembly. We may distance ourselves from others because we feel our place in the group (imagined or real) sets us apart. The pull of the North Node says to develop our own approach, and make choices based on individual values.

North Node in Virgo, South Node in Pisces: With the North Node here, it is time to develop discernment by looking at the finer details of life. Things must be taken down to their component parts, examined, compared and contrasted. Ritual order and service brings growth by making decisions based on conscious understanding.

With the South Node in Pisces, the past may have been a bit of a mixed swirl of feelings and impressions. The tendency could be to retreat into a feeling of chaos through any and all forms of escapism. It is like a disappearing act. The pull of the North Node encourages the individual to come back to the mundane world through conscious activities, work and service.

North Node in Libra, South Node in Aries: With the North Node here, we need to cultivate a sense of peace, beauty and refinement. We benefit by considering the other person's needs over our own and employing the virtue of non-confrontation. Partnerships of all kinds become very important because this placement says *don't go it alone.*

The South Node in Aries suggests a pull toward self-will and narcissistic behavior. That may have been important for development in the past; now the needs have changed. Unity takes precedence over self-seeking.

North Node in Scorpio—South Node in Taurus: With the North Node here, the need it to delve deep into the undercurrent layers of life. Risks must be taken and erotic transformations dared. The occult may be pursued, leaving the mundane behind. We need to merge our energy to create a greater whole. The North Node here also benefits from helping others to develop their own resources.

The South Node in Taurus can pull us back into the material world where we found success in the past. It may be hard to let go of the comfort and indulgences of *the good life,* although a better life for this placement is found in the merging depths of the soul.

North Node in Sagittarius, South Node in Gemini: This placement suggests the need to have a strong sense of meaning and purpose in life. We need something to believe in. Those with the North Node here benefit by traversing distant horizons, expanding their experiences both physically and spiritually. A positive and optimistic outlook feeds the enthusiasm.

The South Node in Gemini can bring over from the past a propensity to dispense energy, flitting from endeavor to endeavor without developing a strong sense of meaning. There can be a lot of talk and not much constructive action. The tendency is to already *know* everything, leaving little to be discovered. The pull of Sagittarius says it is time to find a deeper inner belief.

North Node in Capricorn, South Node in Cancer: The North Node in Capricorn suggests the need to develop a strong and stable sense of self-authority. We have to become capable in our own right, standing as an example to others of containment, reliance and independence. There is benefit gained by acknowledging our sense of healthy ambition and desire to achieve.

The South Node in Cancer pulls us back into the womb of co-dependency. We may feel unable to stand on our own without the support of *mother* in all her various forms (the person, the family, friends, boss, institutions, government support and organizations). The pull of the North Node says it is time to leave this form of security to the past and strike out on our own.

North Node in Aquarius, South Node in Leo: The North Node here suggests the need to develop a sense of unity within a group or organization. Like Prometheus stealing fire to bring creative insights to humankind, the risks and subsequent guilt must be borne. With this Node, we must look to the future of the group, tribe or community and the greater good for all.

The South Node in Leo suggests a pull-back to individual and self-serving endeavors. Once authentic, these no longer serve the growth of the individual but are like a security blanket, protecting us from the rigors of the larger way. The pull of the North Node lures us out of our own self-aggrandizement to focus on the needs of others.

North Node in Pisces, South Node in Virgo: The North Node here suggests the need to melt into the creative and expressive longings of the collective. It could mean becoming an instrument of divine inspiration through healing arts, creativity, literature and spiritual aspirations. The need is to serve a greater whole by reconnecting with the divine.

The South Node in Virgo may resist this merging with the ineffable. It all seems like way too much chaos and way too little order. We may become critical, over judgmental or even lose our sense of compassion. The pull of the North Node is towards the alchemical Arts and away from the separateness of discretion.

North Node in the First House, South Node in the Seventh House: The North Node in the first house indicates an individual that needs to develop his or her own initiative, using energy, ideas and ambition to be a unique person. With the South Node in the seventh, there has been a tendency to rely on others, giving up personal power and gaining a sense of self from people they are with. This Nodal placement needs to strike out independently, identifying less with others and more with self.

North Node in the Seventh House, South Node in the First: The North Node in the seventh suggests that the native needs to develop a sense of symbioses by nurturing his personal one-to-one relationships. The South Node in the first says there is too much independence, autonomy and self-will. This can be balanced by fostering other people's development and immersing in the give and take world of partnerships.

North Lunar Node in the Second, South Lunar Node in the Eighth: The North Lunar Node in the second house indicates someone who needs to develop his or her own support through resources. The task is to become financially independent. The South Node position suggests a past reliance on other people's money, and support (financial or psychological). It may feel easier to be looked after, but a truer sense of self is enhanced by addressing self-survival in the world.

North Node in the Eighth House, South Node in the Second House: The North Node in the eighth house suggests the need to merge energy, take risks and help others find their own sense of self worth. The South Node in the second indicates a past of tangible accumulation and self-oriented values that do not foster generosity. Working on joint projects, merging finances and helping others reach their goals, tangible, psychological or spiritual, will bring fulfillment.

North Node in the Third House, South Node in the Ninth House: The North Node in the third house needs to develop its own ideas through knowledge, education and rational thought processes. Sticking to a routine in the day-to-day environment, without wandering too far afield too often, will help this process. The South Node in the ninth suggests a blind faith in the past that gave a sense of meaning without understanding. Now the native must add knowledge and wisdom to faith.

North Node in the Ninth House, South Node in the Third House: The North Node in the ninth house suggests a need to develop a sense of deep faith through broadening the horizons, exploring other cultures and finding a spiritual significance in life. The South Node in the third house can mean that in the past the powers of the mind were overly developed and have created separation with the sense of faith. This position needs to travel and open the heart to new inner experiences.

North Node in the Fourth House, South Node in the Tenth House: The North Node in the fourth house suggests a need to develop a sense of roots within the self and the power of the soul. This is best done in the spear of the domestic life, in retreat, in the depths of the self. The South Node in the tenth indicates a past public power or fame that now needs to be turned inward. Through privacy and withdrawal, the soul powers are regenerated.

North Node in the Tenth House, South Node in the Fourth House: With the North Node in the tenth house, these natives need to develop their powers in society, nurturing a vocation or career that brings them out of their shell. The South Node in the fourth can spend too much energy in isolated self-reflection. Now the time has come to bring the developed self out into the world.

North Node in the Fifth House, South Node in the Eleventh

House: The North Node in the fifth House suggests the need to develop the creative side of the heart. Through the arts, dance, drama, literature—books they write, pictures they paint, plays they perform—or even through children of the body, the native gains a sense of his or her own specialty. The South Node in the eleventh suggests a past of allowing the desires and will of others to dominate. Here the native must get in touch with his or her own passions and not rely on the opinion or approval of the group.

North Node in the Eleventh House, South Node in the Fifth House: The North Node in the eleventh house indicates the native's need to become involved in a group or collective in some way. The South Node in the fifth house has spent too long on individual creative expression and now needs to integrate it with the creativity of others. Through social awareness and a common cause, a greater sense of self in connection to community is reached.

North Node in the Sixth House, South Node in the Twelfth House: The North Node in the sixth house indicates the need to develop order, structure and ritual routine to gain a richer sense of self. The South Node in the twelfth suggests that in the past, the native spent too much time in daydreams, fantasies and the whims of the collective. Now it's necessary to roll up his or her sleeves, work hard and gain a sense of being through service in the day to day life.

North Node in the Twelfth House, South Node in the Sixth House: The North Node in the twelfth house suggests the need to melt down boundaries and discover the connective nature of all life through empathy, compassion and service. The South Node in the sixth house could have been critical and overly pragmatic in the past. Now the native can best develop himself or herself through opening up to something greater than what is found in the mundane.

The Zero Degree Aries Point

Some people have thousands of reasons why they cannot do what they want to, when all they need is one reason why they can.—Martha Graham

The Zero Degree Aries point, or AP, is the vernal equinox in the tropical zodiac. Mathematically, it is like a planetary node. The AP marks the degree where the sun crosses the equatorial plain going north. Think of it as a Sun/earth node, as opposed to the commonly used Lunar nodes which involve the Sun/earth/Moon.

The Aries Point, or AP, isn't just zero degrees of Aries, give or take a degree of orb. It also links to zero degrees of all the cardinal signs. Every chart—natal, progressed or horary or composite—has the AP at exactly the same zero degrees of Aries, Cancer, Libra and Capricorn, yet each chart will be unique as to house placement and planet contacts these points receive. Any planet or angle in the chart on the AP within a tight orb of 1.5 degrees will give information for a particular kind of achievement and aptitude.

The AP represents a movement from an inner quality to an outer manifestation. It orients us towards the world at large—society, public events and all relationships propelled from the individual to the collective. When a planet or point conjuncts the AP the nature and energy drive of that planet has the added thrust or urge to express collectively. It can represent what the public at large recognize most readily in us, or remembers us for. The AP also can relate to meetings with those public figures who are respected or expert in their field.

0 Aries suggests how our "will to be," or sense of I AM, moves out from the subjective and into manifest reality.

0 Cancer suggests how our need to love and nurture, our sense of "I Feel," moves from the subjective into the world.

0 Libra says, "I relate," suggesting how our drive to interact with others in socially significant ways moves from our inner world and out towards other individuals.

0 Capricorn says, "I produce," suggesting how our urge to bring tangible results moves from "self" to society as a whole.

Sun-AP can mean our energy, vitality and drive seeks to express through society. People see us for our solar qualities and we propel our creative drive into the collective. The famous individual.

Moon-AP suggests that our inner world of feelings, reflections and intuition expresses in public ways, and these qualities are noticed by the collective. The famous psychic.

Mercury-AP can mean our intellect, thoughts and ways of communicating capture the public eye. We are recognized as being witty, bright, mercurial, and clever. The famous writer.

Venus-AP can mean our sensual, accommodating ability to connect and bond with others moves out into a greater social arena. People see us for our capricious, artistic and ingratiating qualities. The famous artist.

Eros-AP suggests our passionate desire for erotic transformation is noticed by the collective. People see our potent energy as tantalizing or threatening, according to their own views. The famous courtesan.

Mars-AP suggests our assertive, direct and action oriented qualities grab the attention of society. We are seen as commanding, raw and imposing. The famous warrior.

Jupiter-AP can mean our leadership qualities, expansiveness, optimism and call for justice capture the attention of the collective. We are seen for our vision, immensity, and joviality. The famous world leader.

Saturn-AP suggests our ability to build tangible results through persistent and sustained effort is highlighted by public acclaim. We are seen for our ambition, caution and pragmatic detail. The famous corporate director.

Chiron-AP suggests renown for our ability to teach, understand, strive for the impossible and restore compassion. We are seen as a healer for those who have lost faith or are in despair. The famous Guru.

Uranus-AP suggests our ability to make sudden changes, rebel against dogmatic convictions and break out of the safety zone is noticed by society. We are seen as surprising, inventive and inspiring. The famous revolutionary.

Neptune-AP suggests the longing for the divine and the desire to merge with the collective unconscious is captured by the projection of society. We are seen as the public want to see us. The famous movie star.

Pluto-AP suggests the ruthless drive for power and control is noticed socially as it wrestles with the need to plumb the depths of the unconscious mind. We are seen for our potent qualities, the dark hero who can be transformed. The famous eccentric.

Ascendant-AP suggests being known for personality traits and interactions in the world. Having famous friends!

Midheaven-AP suggests being known for social achievement through career, mission or profession. Working with famous people!

North Node-AP suggests being known for following the path to the future. Having a famous guide!

South Node-AP suggests being known for redeeming the path of the past. Being a guide to others.

Consider how the AP differs from the MC and the Ascendant:

The ASCENDANT describes the way we put ourselves out into the world: "Hey, this is my personality! This is how I initiate things and assert myself. This is how I look."

Isabel Hickey said the Ascendant was the window through which we view the world and that seems to work both ways. It is often the way the world sees us, on a PERSONAL level. Think of Aries as the natural ruler of the Ascendant and first house with its emphasis on personal self-awareness. This is Me, Here Now!

The MIDHEAVEN is not as personal as the Ascendant. It is public. It has to do with our social standing, career in life, mission or profession. Now, instead of personal appearances (Ascendant.) we are in the realm of PUBLIC APPEARANCES. This is our social identity and often reflects how we interact with "the public" or the collective. The Ascendant is individual identity, the MC is social identity. Think of Capricorn as natural ruler of the MC with the Sea-goat's ambitious, pragmatic and sometimes mystic, social awareness.

The Ascendant is always that moment of ascension, and the MC is a moment of culmination. The AP, however, can occur anywhere in the 365 degrees! It is always 0 Aries but where it falls is unique to the individual chart.

By contrast to the Ascendant and MC, the AP is a solar node. Its energy is about INSTIGATION, beginnings, and action, not in terms of personal needs and drives or even for career or profession, but for Solar manifestation and distinction. The AP makes a statement about how the world sees us! It can indicate the relative "fame" of an individual (or infamy) and how society at large or world events may affect our lives. According to the Uranian School, the AP is also our concept of the world, people in the public life and our approach to manifest reality!

The AP is literally and symbolically the point where the spirit

118

(SUN) enters manifest reality (EARTH). For everyone, that is an ARIES experience, a cardinal experience of action, initiation, inauguration. WHERE that initiation of spirit into matter occurs, is indicated by the house placements of these points. They tell us where we are in relationship to the world at large.

To unravel the meaning the AP in the natal chart, observing the planets, asteroids or points that are connected to it by aspect or transit. What seems to wake up? What does it need? What does it have to offer? Answers to these questions will help understand what the AP means in practical terms, and how that applies to the immediate moment.

The Vertex

"I conclude that all is well," says Oedipus, and that remark is sacred. It echoes in the wild and limited universe of man. It teaches that all is not, has not been, exhausted...It makes of fate a human matter, which must be settled among men.—Albert Camus

What is the vertex?

The vertex is a theoretical point developed by L. Edward Johndro in the 1930s and '40s. It's a very new thing, marking the place in the heavens where the ecliptic—the apparent orbit of the Sun around the earth—crosses the prime vertical—the plane that runs at right angles to the meridian and divides the celestial sphere from front to back. Like the Ascendant and the Lunar Nodes, it is illusory because there is nothing really out there at that point in space—no fixed star, no asteroid, no planet. Still, the vertex can be a potent indicator of timing, of turning points significant in the life.

The vertex falls on the western side of the chart, with the anti-vertex found exactly 180 degrees away, on the eastern side. As with the Ascendant and Midheaven, an exact birth time is necessary to calculate the vertex. There is no point working with it unless there is one. That is the first rule.

What does the word vertex mean?

The word vertex comes from the Latin root word *vertere*, meaning to change, to turn, turn frequently or spin. It also can mean a crowning point, summit, top or crest. Words having this Latin root include vertebrae, (joint, having something to turn on) vertigo (dizzy, disoriented, spun out) vertical (from top to bottom) versatile (doing many things at once, to turn from one thing to another) and verticil (a circular arrangement around a fixed point, a whorl). The common theme here highlights change or movement, from one point to another, where the center remains fixed or the same.

Can mythology reveal anything about the vertex?

Perhaps. The Roman god Vertumnus has roots in the Latin word vertere, to change, turn or spin. Vertumnus was a lesser god of gardens, fruit trees and seasons. Youthful and alluring, he had the power to change himself into various forms, just as the seed changes from root, to branch to leaf to fruit. Vertumnus used this ability in his avid pursuit of the goddess Pomona.

As the myth goes, Vertumnus fell in love with a strikingly beautiful goddess (in some versions nymph) named Pomona. Although she rejected all suitors, he fed his passion with the sight of her by changing his form and passing her gardens daily as a soldier, a harvester, a fisherman, etc. Ignoring him, Pomona remained devoted only to the cultivation of fruit trees. Vertumnus persisted and one day he altered his form to that of an old woman, greeted her with a passionate kiss, and proceeded to enter her gardens.

Vertumnus, (as the matron), talked to the goddess, attempting to convince her of the rewards of relationship and the dangers of rejecting love. The qualities and integrity of the youthful god Vertumnus were discussed. Finally, "she" told Pomona the story of a young man who cruelly took his own life after being spurned by his hard hearted love. He told of how the gods turned the rejecting woman into stone, but still Pomona was not persuaded.

Finally in exasperation, Vertumnus dropped his disguise and stood naked before Pomona in his true form. She thought she was seeing the sun emerge from behind the clouds and in the glorious light of Vertumnus, she opened her heart and reciprocated his love. Together still, they attend the gardens and fruit tress of the countryside.

The theme of this myth centers on a seemingly chance moment where an outstanding event occurs. To Pomona, it was like an epiphany, a sudden turn of fate, a radical awakening of perception. To Vertumnus, it was at first a well planned strategy, then finally an act of spontaneous desperation. Imagine his surprise when Pomona finally received him!

Love, relationship and union are highlighted here, not just in the desire of Vertumnus, but also in the story he told of the young man's rejection and the tragic consequences that followed. The imagery of the gardens, fruit and vine add to the feeling of ripeness, an event finally ready to happen, a fruitful experience.

What does it mean astrologically?

The vertex appears as a sensitive point linked to fateful encounters with others, seemingly sudden epiphanies, turning points in life and a destiny over which we have no apparent control. Activated, it can synchronize with an experience of another whose effect registers as some degree of profound or extraordinary.

A strongly placed natal vertex (conjunct the horizon, in close aspect to a personal planet, in a critical degree or in the degree of the nodes) can indicate more consistent results. What activates the Vertex? Three things, as always—transits, people and places.

Transits to the vertex can bring inner and outer events corresponding to a pivotal point, significant encounter with another or a sudden change of perception. The transiting planet activates the symbolism of the vertex, coinciding with a major or minor event. Keeping orbs tight and sticking mainly to the conjunction will bring more consistent results. A transiting conjunction from Mars would likely be more noticeable than a transiting trine from Uranus, although sometimes that is not the case. The magnitude of the effect depends on the prominence of the vertex itself, its relationship to other factors in the chart and the occurrence of other transits, commensurate or disparate. Along with transits, students are encouraged to consider progressions, converse progressions and directions.

Meetings with significant people, as seen through synastry and composite charts, may also link strongly to the vertex. (Think of people as constant transits.) When one person's inner planets (Sun through to Jupiter), angles, nodes, vertex or certain Arabic parts conjunct the vertex, there can be a feeling of fate, destiny, rightness or wrongness about the encounter. Something in the contact with that person may have the ability to create profound change in the native, over a long or short period of time. The change may be perceived as pleasing or acrimonious, the conjunction often reflecting the former, the opposition the later.

Our location on the planet can awaken the vertex as seen through relocation charts and astro-carto-graphy. When we relocate, the vertex may become more prominent by changing house or aspect to an angle. The relocation vertex can signify places where meaningful encounters of a particular nature seem to happen more consistently.

What about the sign and house position of the vertex?

The house positions of the vertex/anti-vertex can offer clues as to where we may experience turning points, meetings with destiny or fateful encounters in life. As noted earlier, the vertex falls usually between the fifth and the eight houses, on the western side of the chart, with the anti-vertex 180 degrees opposition.

In the fifth/eleventh house axis, there could be a propensity to experience fateful romantic or creative encounters (fifth house) through contacts with friends or groups (eleventh house). In the sixth/twelfth house axis, the turning point, or spin out, could effect our day by day living, or our link between psyche and soma (sixth house) through contact with those in the helping professions, those less fortunate or through dreams and creative fantasies (twelfth house). In the seventh/first house axis, sudden epiphanies could radically effect socially significant partnerships (seventh house) through an experience of projecting ourselves out into the world (first house). In the eighth/second house axis, destiny may arrive in the form of an erotic encounter or intense research (eighth house) perpetrated by a desire for pleasure, security or peace (second house).

The vertex/anti-vertex by sign can signify the way we may experience activation to this axis. Aries/Libra could indicate issues between personal will and sharing, where Taurus/Scorpio may be about security verses risk. Gemini/Sagittarius could contrast knowledge and vision, where Cancer/Capricorn could emphasize protection verses enterprise. The Leo/Aquarius axis might highlight self-expression as opposed to group participation where the Virgo/Pisces might compare structured boundaries and limitless longing.

The Vertex and Aptitude

The vertex is a point in the horoscope that can indicate a sense of destiny working through another person or outstanding event. It may be stimulated by transits, progressions or directions, other people (synastry/composite) or a change of location. The house and sign position can offer clues as to where the change or turning point may take place and in what way. Watching the vertex as it is activated in the chart can determining the relative value as indicator of direction and major choice. Knowledge, insight, and inspiration usually arrive at such times. After all, we never know when Vertumnus might enter our garden in the guise of someone else, offering an unexpected turn of fate!

Arabic Parts: From Passion to Fortune

The Arabic Points, or Parts, are based on the solar degree on the Ascendant and cover an array of topics from *most illustrious friends* to *most perilous year*. Obviously, some of these points will not be relevant for everyone. Some, however, especially the Part of Fortune, can give us a glimpse of ourselves that we otherwise would not recognize.

To use the formulas below, an exact and accurate birth time must be known because they often incorporate fast changing degrees like the lunar position, Ascendant and Descendant. If the time is in question, then good results can be obtained by using the Ascendant at 0 Aries.

Part of Fortune (Fortuna)

The Fortuna is calculated by adding the Ascendant to the Moon by degree and sign and then subtracting the Sun. This can be done instantly on a computer program or fairly quickly by hand. Example: Ascendant = 10 Leo 15, Moon = 20 Scorpio 16 and the Sun = 3 Taurus 07. The Fortuna would be (10.15 plus 20.16 = 30.31 – 3.7 = 27 degrees 24/ Leo(5) plus Scorpio (8) = 13 (Aries) – Taurus (2) = Aquarius (11) making the Part of Fortune 27 Aquarius 24) Just remember, the signs are not linear, but move around in an endless circle. You may have to subtract the 12 signs, or 30 degrees, to get the correct result.

This point is important for finding our sense of joy and inner fulfillment. If the Part of Fortune is not being activated in some way, our whole hearts will not be involved. Consider the sign and house placement and also the aspect degree to discover the depths of the Fortuna.

The brief descriptions that follow are a springboard for your further thought and contemplation. Whole stories can be made around the loves and longings of the Fortuna by sign, house and aspect. The student is encouraged to amass his or her own notes.

Fortuna in Aries needs to feel *adventurous, questing, challenging, leading and winning.*

Fortuna in Taurus *needs to feel sensual, practical in natural ways with tangible results.*

Fortuna in Gemini *needs to feel intellectual, communicative, teaching and learning.*

Fortuna in Cancer *needs to feel needed, nurturing, protective and comforting.*

Fortuna in Leo *needs to feel special, honored, creative and flamboyant.*

Fortuna in Virgo *needs to feel discerning, articulate, detailed and analyzing.*

Fortuna in Libra *needs to feel fair, balanced, beautiful and harmonizing.*

Fortuna in Scorpio *needs to feel intense, deeply entrenched, powerful and in control.*

Fortuna in Sagittarius *needs to feel expansive, exploratory, meaningful and energized.*

Fortuna in Capricorn *needs to feel ambitious, productive, achieving and recognized.*

Fortuna in Aquarius *needs to feel detached, knowledgeable, humanitarian and free.*

Fortuna in Pisces *needs to feel merged, understood, compassionate and connected.*

Part of Passion

Another significant Arabic Point is the Part of Passion. It is found by adding the Ascendant to Mars and then subtracting the Sun. Example: Ascendant 28 Leo (5) 15 plus Mars 8 Capricorn (10) 05 = 36 degrees 20 (15) minus 1 Gemini (3) 19 = 33 degrees 01 (12) or 3 Aries (1) 01. This shows how we move to the next sign if there are more than 30 degrees showing (33 degrees 1 minus 30 degrees of the zodiac equals 3 degrees 01 in the next sign).

The Part of Passion appears to be a sensitive point related to energy, drive and enthusiasm for adventure. This is more the passion of the soul for creative expression than the passion of the heart for love and romance. It is an interesting point to watch by lunation, transit and direction. Also, we can watch the effect of this point in the synastry charts of those who work with us on joint projects of any kind.

Part of Increase

The Arabic Part of Increase is interesting as well. It is derived by adding the Ascendant to Jupiter and then subtracting the Sun. This can be a point to watch for the attraction of abundance, and what, by house and sign, needs to be stimulated to awaken this Point.

Part of Sudden Advancement

The Part of Sudden Advancement is a curious position, in that it includes, not Uranus as we might expect, but Saturn. This could be in accordance with Saturn's original rulership over Aquarius, or simply reflect the possible wealth hidden in the symbolism of the Titan god. The point is found by adding the Ascendant to the Sun and subtracting Saturn (unless Saturn is combust the Sun—in that case, substitute Jupiter). It may be interesting to experiment with Uranus as a substitute as well.

All these Arabic parts may be important in timing events and can awaken strongly by transits, lunations and particularly transits by the progressed Moon. The Fortuna can show up in surprising ways in the synastry of family charts and is certainly a point integral to a sense of happiness. These intriguing sensitive points would make an excellent research project for those who feel drawn.

Midpoints that Make a Difference

Midpoints in the natal chart represent a merging or combining of planets and points where they meet, abstractly, halfway. They are plotted by finding the midway mark between them. If a person's Sun is 1 Aries and another person's Moon is 1 Leo, the Sun/Moon midpoint will fall in two opposing places. The nearer midpoint places the it at 1 Gemini, and the farther midpoint places it directly opposite at 1 Sagittarius.

Because the horoscope is spherical and not linear, there will always be two midpoints exactly 180 degrees apart for every combination of planets. One will form a shorter arc and the other a longer one. The shorter arc is generally considered stronger.

Because it is not often easy to see the midpoints at a glance, the quickest way to derive them is to reduce the points to a degree between 0 and 360, add them together and divide by two. (20 Taurus becomes 50; 18 Aquarius becomes 318. Together they are 368/2 = 184 or 4 Libra.) Because the closest distance between Taurus and Aquarius is Aries, the opposition would be used: 4 Aries.

The signs translate into degrees as follows:

Aries	0
Taurus	30
Gemini	60
Cancer	90
Leo	120
Virgo	150
Libra	180
Scorpio	210
Sagittarius	240
Capricorn	270
Aquarius	300
Pisces	330

All midpoints are worthy of study and research, although some jump out as being more aligned with talents and aptitude in the natal chart. Consider midpoints to the Sun, Mercury, Venus, North Node and Saturn, as well as points with the natal second, sixth and tenth house rulers. Consider the depositor of the Fortuna (the ruler of the sign it is found in), the Fortuna itself and ruler of any stelliums by house or sign. The following list is brief—a springboard for further investigation. The best thing to do is to make your own list, starting with the Sun. Think about what each planet particularly needs and has to offer in terms of aptitude and talents, then consider how they might interact.

For example, the Sun in Gemini in the tenth house may want to teach, write and be recognized for communication skills. This Sun may offer the impetus and curiosity necessary to follow such a path. Mercury may be in Cancer—more intuitive and prone to work through thoughts and feelings methodically. This Mercury may have a vivid imagination and be able to work long hours at a home/office. Together, the midpoint may describe the combination of imagination and writing skills, turning facts to fiction in the creation of novels, exploratory research or creative visual arts. Having this midpoint on an angle, another natal planet or activated by transit or progression will awaken the quality further.

Take the time to study your own chart in this way, planet by planet, and come up with a personal table of midpoint meanings. Examples:

Sun/Mercury: Speaking, writing, communications, travel on the job.

Sun/Venus: Artistic flare, charisma, enchantment

Sun/Mars: Enthusiasm, self-employment, healthy assertion.

Sun/Jupiter: Success, optimism, opportunity.

Sun/Saturn: Recognition through hard work, long hour and dedication.

Sun/Node: Help from others, inspiration, new possibilities.

Moon/Mercury: Adept writing talent, especially fiction.

Moon/Jupiter: Success in material enterprises, luck

Mercury/Venus: Success through charm, the arts, diplomacy, journalism.

Mercury/Mars: Critical thinking, debate, battle of words

Mercury/Jupiter: Communication effecting many, scientific breakthrough, legal success.

Venus/Jupiter: Ability to influence others, negotiate, win favor, instill confidence.

Venue/Node: Relationships that bring opportunity, working with significant others.

Mars/Jupiter: Climbing to the top, winning, self-authority, self-employment.

Jupiter/Uranus: Unexpected "peak" experience that can change life direction.

Jupiter/MC: New career, mission or profession or success and respect there.

Saturn/Node: success with others hard won, difficulty with others leads to appreciation.

Fixed Stars as Signs of Destiny

Fixed stars are actual stars as opposed to planets, which are wandering stars. They were used extensively in ancient astrology; now, probably because of their sensational and sometimes sever interpretations, they are not as popular. It is challenging to find an objective interpretation of a *malefic* fixed star like Serpentis that, in 19-22 Scorpio, is designated *the accursed degree of the accursed sign.*[33]

Another problematic aspect of the fixed stars is that they number in the thousands. The question arises (just as it does with the thousands of asteroids and dozens of Arabic Parts and midpoints) concerning which ones should be plotted and used. These are valid points for research and, in the interim, one can watch the significant fixed stars designated by the ancients to record meaningful results. It may be of more benefit than first realized.

Margaret Hone,[34] and other pioneering teachers of the last century felt the fixed stars worthy of consideration, especially if a natal body made a conjunction or opposition to one of them. They are then said to increase the significance of the natal body and also contribute the star's character to its expression.

Certain fixed stars are noted as signs of talent. The list on the next two pages is provided as an introduction only. The student interested in this area of astrology is encouraged to do his or her own research and further reading. (See the listing of fixed stars on pages 129-132.)

Asteroids Related to Aptitude and Inspiration

". . . The 'minor planets' are by no means minor in their action." Demetra George

There are so many asteroids out there between Venus and Jupiter, and Centaurs between Saturn and Neptune, KBO's and now, with the discovery of Sedna, possibly myriad more Ort Could objects. If we plot them all in the natal chart, it would be filled in, blacked out. The point in working with the asteroids is to choose those significant to the immediate question or investigation. If the chart is being evaluated for relationship, for example, asteroid Eros, Psyche, Amor, Sappho, Cupido and Adonis might be added,

Star	Longitude (1990)	Declination (1990)	Planet Corr.	Aptitude
Achird	09TA27	47N20	Sa/Ve	Interior design, architecture, curator, landscaping, art therapy, art history
Algenib	09AR09	15N11		Oratory skills
Aldebaran (Hyades)	9GE39	05S28	Ma	Science, medicine, biology, research, fine arts, martial arts, athletics, legal abilities, literature, creativity, good business sense, occult studies
Algol (CaputAlgol)	26TA02	22N26	Sa/Ma/Ur	Crisis counseling, therapist, writer
Alhena	08CA58	06S45	Ve/Ju	Science, fine arts, creative expression, musical ability, martial arts, athletics, military, mariner or marine studies, good negotiator, fashion design, mediumistic, psychic ability
Alkes	23VI41	18S18		Landscaping, architecture, design, engineering
Alphecca	12CS18	26N42		Botany, astrology, athletics, martial arts, leadership, medicine, literature, music and arts, psychic ability
Atlas (Pleiades)	00GE13	03N55	Mo/Ju	Helping professions, real estate, travel agent
Atria	20SA54	69S02		Scientific ability
Asellus/ Australis	08LE35	00N05	Su/Ma	Sports, martial arts and military pursuits, government work, organizational skills

Star	Longitude (1990)	Declination (1990)	Planet Corr.	Aptitude
Asellus Borealis	07LE24	03N11	Su/Ma	Financier, banking, stocks, bonds, speculation and investments, energetic reformer, military, athletics and martial arts, heroic leader, schools, amusement, entertainment, occult studies
Bellatrix	20GE57	06N21		Medicine , surgeon, athletics, martial arts, military, electrical engineering, occult studies
Capella	21GE51	46N00	Ve	Literary/poetry ability, political interests, public position, research skills, teaching and education, sports, military, inventive
Castor (Apollo)	20CA06	10N06	Me/Ju	Publishing, writing and public speaking (better writer than speaker), acting abiliity (silent roles), mariner or marine studies, lawyers, horse training/breeding, occult studies, philosophy, psychic ability
Hyadum I	05GE48	15N37		Athletics, military, martial arts, literary ability, inventive, philosophy, psychic ability often unconscious
Hyadum II	06GE52	17N32		Political skills
Kitalpha	23AQ43	05N14		Veterinary skills

Star	Longitude (1990)	Declination (1990)	Planet Corr.	Aptitude
Markab	23PI21	19N24	Me/Ma	Martial arts, sports, athletics
Menkalinan (Alanz)	29GE46	21N31	Ju/Ma/Ve	Social work, education, teaching and raising young
Menkent	12SC18	36S21		Medicine and healing, divination, construction, foreman, astronomy
Metallah	06TA52	29N34		Architecture and design, legal ability
Mira	01TA31	02S59		Problem solving skills
Nath (El Nath)	22GE26	05N23	Ma	Success comes late in life, science, good speaker, debater, good in business and partnerships, occult studies, philosophy
Pollux (Hercules)	23CA05	06N41	Ma	Peculiar occupations, promotion and and honor with risk of fall, excellent linguist, mariner or marine biology, electronics, martial arts, sparing, good business partner, philosophy, psychic ability
Regulus (Kalb)	29LE42	00N28	Ju/Ma	Astrology, occult studies, indicates promotion to high acclaim, even from lowest position, artistic ability, natural leader
Sirius	13CA57	39S35	Ma/Ju	Gain through friends, fine arts and creative self-expression, metallurgical engineer, lawyer, government position,

Star	Longitude (1990)	Declination (1990)	Planet Corr.	Aptitude
				custodian, curator, guardian, occult interests, organizational skills, business partnerships/opportunities, dog trainer/breeder
Spica (Azimech)	23LI42	02S03	Ve/Ma	Fine arts, responsible position, artist/painter, honor and promotion, scientist, sculptor, musician, inventive, mediumistic, occult studies
Unukalhai (Serpens)	22SC40	06N25	Ma/Sa	Craftsmanship, agruculture
Vega	15CP19	38N47		Political abilities, statesman, occult interests, influential position, scientific interests, fine arts, music, acting, business partnerships
Vindemiatrix	09LI48	16N12	Sa/Me	Mechanical, engineering and inventive ability, successful business partnerships
Zuben Elgenubi	14SC57	00N20	Ma/Sa	Telepathic/empathic skills

and others as well. Name asteroids are always interesting to find and plot. When it comes to aptitude, talents and skills, there are asteroids that can, when conjunct or in significant aspect to a planet or point, add insightful information to the delineation. They also can be relevant to watch by transit and progression.

How are they considered? Mostly they will show up as red flags, highlighters of talents and indications of interest. If Hephaestus is conjunct the Sun, there could be an interest in craft, blacksmithing and working with hand tools. If asteroid Shakespeare is conjunct the fifth house cups, work in the theater, playwriting or acting could be a form of creative expression. Hygiea conjunct the Moon could indicate working in women's health. Icarus to Mercury might write or speaking for out for freedom or adventure. The following is an alphabetical list including some of the many asteroids that can link to career, mission and aptitude. Use is as a guideline to considering professional choices in natal, progressed and returned charts. This list is in no way comprehensive. Asteroid 433 Eros receives a more comprehensive review at the end.

1862 Apollo is the dazzling "lord of light," a solar deity. His origins are diverse, his personalities multiple. He is the god of light yet not the sun itself. He is the god of creativity and leader of the Muses, yet also the god of sudden death. Music, marksmanship and divination are his domain. He never shunned battle or the chance to compete for domination and killed many a foe, yet he also was a shepherd god, guardian of the vulnerable flock and herd. If Apollo is found on one of the angles or in aspect to a personal planet, the healing arts, music, divination, sport, archery, and adventure may weave quite naturally into the aptitudes of the native. One client the Apollo conjunct Mercury in Taurus in the seventh was a shiatsu therapist. Another, with Apollo on the Ascendant in Aries competes in triathlons.

4581 Asclepius is the god of medicine. Son of Apollo and Coronis, Asclepius was raised by Chiron where he learned the healing arts. He was renown as a surgeon, pharmacist, maker of potions (including love potions), spells and incantations, and also used the blood of the gorgon, Medusa to produce miraculous cures. When he offended Zeus, he was destroyed by a thunderbolt, but Zeus later honored him by placing him in the stars as part of the constellation

Ophiuchus. Hippocrates is said to be his descendant. When Asclepius is in close aspect to an inner planet or point, medicine, particularly traditional western approaches such as surgery, medical researching, teaching positions and specialist techniques come to the foreground. One client with Asclepius in Scorpio conjunct the Vertex in the sixth house was a Veterinary nurse who experienced major turning points in her life through her profession.

1 Ceres is an earth mother goddess who was worshiped for her control over the harvest, the seasons and what the earth brought forth. Her tie with her daughter Persephone is potent. The girl is like an extension of herself until she is abducted by Pluto. As mother goddess, Ceres presides over all phases of growth, nurturing and animal husbandry. When Ceres is in aspect to a natal planet, angel or significant point, the theme of nurturing carries over into the expression of the other planets. It can manifest as a desire to work with families, childcare, food industries (from growing to serving), animal care and medicine, and welfare. Many clients involved with agriculture and nurseries have prominent Circes. A bacteriologist who incubated culture medium to find specific antibiotic agents for pathogens had Circes conjunct mars in the sixth house. One client with Ceres trine the Moon in Cancer was a breast-feeding counselor.

34 Circe was an enchantress, a witch of great power who lived on a beautiful, uncharted island. She wove dangerous and terrible spells, and also ones that gave healing and love. The daughter of Helios (the Sun-consciousness) and Perse (the daughter of Okeanos-unconscious waters), she is celebrated for her knowledge of magic and the use of herbs to heal and to transform. When Circe is significantly placed, the mixing of elements for creative purpose, be they pharmaceuticals, paints, or cuisine, may be important. Witchcraft and the Druid arts are also indicated here and such themes may be portrayed in the profession. Master of color and vision, Pablo Picasso, had Asteroid Circe conjunct the sun exact in Scorpio in the fourth house. Two current clients working in the Druid arts have Circe conjunct Sun and Mars respectively. Madame Curie, Nobel Prize winning Chemist and brilliant intellectual had Circe conjunct the North Lunar Node and the Vertex in Virgo in the seventh house.

1864 Daedalus was an Athenian and worked very hard as a craftsman, inventor and engineer. He designed and built the labyrinth under King Minos' castle in Crete which housed the dreaded Minotaur. His skills also had something to do with the creations of the Minotaur. It was Daedalus that designed the wooden cow that Pasiphae, Minos' wife, crouched in to couple with the prize bull. Daedalus was upwardly mobile, ambitious, insightful, inventive and original. This asteroid in the natal chart can indicate an area where there is talent and skill in crafts and working with the hands. Famous architect and designer, Frank Lloyd Wright, had Daedalus conjunct Venus in Gemini.

2212 Hephaestus was the son of Hera, some say with Zeus and some say on her own, parthenogenetically, to spite Zeus for the birth of Athene. Hephaestus was the god of the forge, gifted in his ability to create intricately beautiful works of art and service, although they were not modeled after his own likeness. Hephaestus was hard wording, industrious, humorless, homely and crippled. He uses his brute force to forge implements of battle and thunderbolts for Zeus. He worked with iron, Mars's metal, and created the finest crafts, teaching his skills to mankind. He was an ingenious inventor who had the honor and respect of most the Olympians. One client who was a farrier by trade had Hephaestus conjunct the Sun in Gemini in the tenth house.

69230 Hermes is the Ancient Greek's Mercury. Born form the adulterous union of Zeus and Maia, Hermes is unique in that, of all the offspring of Zeus, his jealous wife Hera did not hate him. Some even had it that she suckled him herself, an unheard of act of acceptance. Hermes's exuberant qualities were evident right from birth when he leaped from his crib, made the first lyre from a turtle shell and proceeded to steal his bother's cattle making him buy them back! He achieved all this before his first sunset! He is the god of god of travel, shepherds, commerce, weights and measures, the written and the spoken word, athletics and thieves. He is associated with alchemy and is the herald of the Olympians. He also guides souls down into the underworld. Hermes in aspect to a personal planet or angle could bring any of his attributes to the foreground, especially shrewdness. Sir Isaac Newton had Hermes conjunct Capricorn in the third house and Comedian Richard Pryor has Hermes conjunct the Moon in Capricorn in the tenth house.

10 Hygiea is the goddess of health and welfare with whom the word 'hygiene' originates. Hygiea is usually depicted with a serpent drinking from a cup held in her hand. This has become the internationally recognized symbol of Pharmacopeias, where the bowl represents medicine and the snake potency. Hygiea is associated with the maintenance of health, specializing in prevention and well being. When Hygiea is strongly placed with an inner planet or angle, it indicates a link to the medical professions, health concerns, research and study and general health care. It is a strong indication of physical fitness. Louis Pasteur, noted chemist and physician who made sweeping discoveries in the field of medicine and immunology had Hygiea conjunct his IC in Aquarius.

1566 Icarus is Daedalus's son who, ignoring his father's warning not to fly too close to the sun, lost his feathered wings, plummeted to the sea and drowned. This asteroid can be a little extreme though it does represent an attempt to escape oppression. It is the impulse to get out of unfair situations or go for liberating goals that others tell us are impossible. It doesn't have to always be "crash and burn". Icarus set free can be vivid inspiration. Otherwise, he is like a wild bird caged. When this asteroid is in aspect to personal planets or points there can be a restless desire for freedom, to soar or to escape. With this energy comes a free spirit both creative and potentially destructive. Stirring Russian ballet dancer Vaslav Nijinsky, known for his extremes of energy and fiery performances, had Icarus conjunct Jupiter in Aquarius the natal third house. One client who is a fireman and part of an emergency rescue squad has Icarus in Sagittarius conjunct Mercury in the tenth house.

3 Juno is primarily the goddess of marriage and maternity. In pre-Hellenistic times she was worshiped outside the context of marriage presiding over all stages of womanhood- maiden, mother, crone. Later, she was merged with the cult of Zeus and became his wife. Basically, she was used as bridge between a matriarchal cult and a patriarchal one. What she stands for now is the inner marriage of animus and anima in every individual. A significantly placed Juno adds a feeling of commitment to whatever planet is touched. Partnerships, contractual agreements, procreations, artistic creation and social rituals are accented. One client who is a psychotherapist working specifically with relationship counseling has Juno conjunct Mercury/Chiron/Saturn/Mars in the sixth house conjunct the Descendant.

3811Karma prompts the meaning gleaned from Hindu or Buddhist "consequences of a person's actions". Fate. Destiny. However, the word originally referred to the simple act of "doing". In that "taking of action" we have a RESULT—consequences which will change our destiny, but Karma isn't the destiny, it is the action that leads to it. The steps we take. In this sense, asteroid 3811 Karma is, by house, sign and aspect, about doing that which must be done. Albert Einstein had asteroid Karma conjunct Saturn in Taurus in the tenth house suggesting that his "work" would be exacting, productive and highly recognized.

1181 Lilith The meaning of Lilith is dark, mysterious and complex, like the mythic figure herself. Once the handmaiden of Inanna, Sumerian goddess of love, she represented sexual initiation and transformation through divine union. In her feminine, potent sexuality and autonomy, Lilith was venerated. Then, she fell. A representation of the dark feminine, Lilith has the capacity to bring spiritual illumination, though she has been repressed, loathed and relegated to the unconscious by patriarchal society. When Lilith is conjunct a personal planet or point, honoring her through the nature of that planet is vital. Lilith represents a kind of emancipation from gender limitations, a freedom and autonomy unrivaled by Aries. When this asteroid is significantly place, one needs to translate her powers of individuality and self-direction into the related aspect of life. Author, astrologer and powerhouse of a woman, considered Mother of the New Age, Madame Blavatsky had Lilith conjunct the North Lunar Node in Leo in her second house. Lilith also formed a yod, inconjunct her MC in Pisces and Neptune in Capricorn on the Descendant.

4386 Lust is about joy, beauty and enthusiasm for becoming. It is a 'Lust for Life' and passion for connection. Lust can also haves feelings of hunger and driving intensity if those desires are not met. When the asteroid is in close aspect to a personal planet or point, it can mean that what that planet represents needs to be experienced with enthusiasm and elation. An infusion of elation can well up through the activation of the planet contacted when it is expressing within the nature of the sign and house placement. Several clients who exhibit an extreme passion for their profession have Lust conjunct their MC, or MC rulers.

The Muses

The Muses were once deities of Spring. Like Nymphs, they were worshiped near lakes, waterfalls and sacred pools. Slowly they changed to demigoddesses, presiding over memory and then poetic and artistic inspiration. They were most noted for their choir and for their songs. They also had the gift of prophesy. Hesiod said they knew "what is, what was and what will be". He describes their voices as bewitching, something that pleased their father Zeus immensely.

Being a muse is a real job to this day. Fashion designers employ them for inspiration. These employees are always women and their sole purpose is to float around and smile, and sigh and enthuse and encourage. They are beautiful, graceful and often have flowing hair and soft eyes. Sometimes they indicate a design or piece that pleases them by drawing little hearts next to it. Yes, it's a real job and apparently well paid. The personification of the Muses is a wonderful creative motivation. It awakens the soul to act.

When a Muse asteroid is placed in close aspect to a personal planet or point, the nature of her attributes may be passed on to the native. Certainly, exploring the academic or artistic themes suggested by the Muse would bring a feeling of enthusiasm and fulfillment.

62 Erato is the muse of poetry, particularly love sonnets and erotic (transformational) themes. She is also known for mimicry and impersonations. Actress Vivian Leigh has asteroid Erato exact on her natal Sun in Scorpio in the sixth house. Novelist John Steinbeck had asteroid Erato conjunct his North Lunar Node and the Moon in Scorpio. Poet W.B. Yeats had Erato in Aquarius conjunct his natal Moon.

27 Euterpe is the muse of lyric and music, especially the guitar, flute and other wind instruments. She inspires creativity through the joys and pleasures of playing song. Elvis Presley had asteroid Euterpe conjunct his North Lunar Node in Capricorn. Joni Mitchell has this asteroid conjunct her Mars in Gemini.

22 Kalliope is the most honored of the muses. She is called 'Fair

138

voice' and that may mean more her skills in arbitration and persuasion that musical. She is known for her eloquence and epic poetry. Frank Abignale Jr., con artist and one of the most persuasive people alive, has Kallipoe in Leo exactly conjunct natal Mars.

84 Klio is the muse of history and heroic poetry. She introduced the Phoenician alphabet to the Greeks and is the mother of Hyacinth. Pulitzer Prize-winning historical fiction writer, James Michener, had asteroid Klio in Leo, exactly opposite his Aquarius Sun/Mercury conjunction.

56 Melete is one of the original three muses. She is linked to memory, art and meditation. Writer Mart Twain had asteroid Melete conjunct his South Lunar Node in Scorpio in the first house. Singer and actress Barbara Streisand has Melete in Taurus conjunct Saturn.

18 Melpomene is the muse of tragedy and melodrama, an inspiration to thespians. The famous mime artist, Marcel Marceau had this asteroid conjunct his Moon in Taurus together with the muse of mime, Polyhymnia. Ly de Angeles, author, performing artist, director and producer has Melponmene exact on her North Lunar Node in Pisces in the third house.

57 Mnemosyne is the mother of the nine muses. She is associated with memory. John Lennon has asteroid Mnemosyne on the midpoint between natal Sun and North Lunar Node (conjunct both) in Libra in the twelfth house. Joni Mitchell has Mnemosyne conjunct her 0 degree Aries Point.

33 Polyhymnia is the muse of sacred hymn or choir. She is more serious, studying geometry, mime and meditation. John Lennon had asteroid Polyhymnia exact on his first house Mercury in Scorpio. Mime artist, Marcel Marceau, had this asteroid conjunct his moon in Taurus.

81 Terpsichore is the muse of the dance, choirs or chorus in theater and of lyric poetry. She is truly inspirational to the souls she touches. Dancer and creative artist, Isadora Duncan, had asteroid Terspichore conjunct her North Lunar Node in Aquarius.

23 Thalia is the muse of comedy, pastoral poetry and agricultural festivals. Actor Jeff Goldblum has asteroid Thalia conjunct his natal Moon in Sagittarius. Vivian Leigh, staring in the film based in the rural South, "Gone With the Wind," had asteroid

Thalia and asteroid Eros in Libra conjunct the natal Vertex in the sixth house. The film certainly was a turning point in her life. (See The Vertex) Marcel Marceau had asteroid Thalia in Capricorn opposite the Ascendant.

30 Urania is the Greek muse of the stars—Astronomy and Astrology. She was also know for skills in precognition. Celebrated astrologer Marc Edmund Jones had asteroid Urania conjunct his MC/Moon/Saturn stellium in Leo. Astrologer/author Robert Hand has Urania opposite his Mercury/Venus conjunction in Sagittarius. Lois Rodden, astrologer, author and founder of AstroDatabank research, had Urania conjunct the North Lunar Node in Gemini. Madame Blavatsky, author, astrologer and founder of the Theosophical Society had Urania conjunct the Moon in Libra.

3361 Orpheus, taught by Apollo, was the greatest musician of his time. According to the Ancient Greeks, his lyre and his singing voice would calm wild beasts. It saved the Argonauts form the deadly lure of the Sirens, and even evoked trees and rocks to uproot and dance.. When Orpheus' wife, Eurydice, was killed by a poisonous snake, he used his songs to charm Cerberus, guardian of the underworld, and persuade Hades to return her to the land of the living. There was one stipulation though. She was to follow him out of the underworld and he was not to look back. He, sadly, looked back just before they were free and he lost her all over again. His mourning was so deep that he was eventually was dismembered by Maenads to silence his grief. Some say he was then reunited with Eurydice where he played for her endlessly in the underworld. Orpheus conjunct a personal planet or point may suggest musical aptitude, and at the lease, powers of persuasion. One client particularly adept at both has Orpheus in Pisces conjunct Venus in the twelfth house.

1143 Odysseus was one of the heroes of the Trojan war, the king of Ithica and a great strategist. He was astute, intellectual, cunning and a fluent public speaker. Apparently, the ruse of the "Trojan Horse" was his idea. Although victorious at Troy, it took him ten years to return home—a totally of twenty years away from his wife Penology. These adventures where told of in Homer's Odyssey. He had several offspring with the witch, Circe, and many encounters with gods, demons and monsters before he returned to Ithica. When Odysseus is in aspect to a personal planets or point, an aptitude for strategy, intellectual pursuits, public speaking, sailing, adventuring and the art of war (military, martial arts or even computer games) may be prominent. Aviator Amelia Earhart had Odysseus exactly opposite her Ascendant in Scorpio. Like Homer's Odysseus, Amelia was also lost on her heroic journeys.

2 Pallas Athene is a warrior, protective, supportive and reportedly asexual. She also was, at heart, very much her father's daughter. Leaping from the wound in Zeus's head after Hephaestus, or some say Prometheus, split it with an axe, Athene was born full grown, dressed in golden armor and screaming a war cry. She proceeded to protect heroic men, guard the city of Athens and was worshiped as the goddess of war-craft, strategy, craftsmanship and wisdom. When Pallas Athene is aspect to a significant point or planet in the natal chart, you get an involvement with intelligence in all its forms: strategy, the art of war, marshal arts, political activism and a propensity for gold or silversmithing, and the law. Winston Churchill had Pallas Athene conjunct his North Lunar Node in Aries in the seventh house.

4450 Pan brings something very earthy, very natural to any planet or point he touches. He's no "Victorian" when it comes to sensations and sensual pleasure. Pan brings a link with the instinctual nature and couples it with a kind of wily pleasure. On the Ascendant, Pan gives the body robust strength, added libido and sharp instinct. He is raw and vital and knows nature's ways. He is a seducer of the innocent, and the knowledgeable as well. He is one hell of a romp, metaphorical or otherwise. He is natural and fertile—a nature spirit, instinctual, rustic, sexual, potent. He is not shy. He is not a child. Pan loves music and dance, reverie, sex and celebration. When conjunct a personal planet, these traits and talents may come to the foreground. Muhammad Ali has Pan conjunct Jupiter in Gemini in the tenth house.

55 Pandora was a gift from Zeus to Prometheus, a kind of punishment for humankind because they had his divine fire. Prometheus politely declined the gift but his brother, Epimetheus said, "yes please." Pandora came with a box, which was not to be opened. She also came with a big dose of curiosity. She opened the box and out flew all the evils and destruction imaginable, yet also contained in the box was the Star of Hope. Pandora means the "All

Gifted One." She received gifts from all the gods on Mt. Olympus when they made her and she has much to offer, if one can handle the disruption that goes with it. Pandora in a significant position adds curiosity, restlessness, vivacity and excitement. She adds a particular nuance, related to sign and house, that is zany, outspoken and eccentric. Audacity. One client with Pandora conjunct the Ascendant in Aquarius had changed majors many times until she discovered psychology. Now, as a psychotherapist, she opens all kinds of boxes, pushes all kinds of buttons, releasing demons and plagues, as well as stars of hope.

1809 Prometheus stole fire from Zeus and gave it to mankind so he would no longer be groping around in the dark. It was a gift, intended to proffer creativity and enlightenment. Of course, he was punished for his charity. Prometheus is a metaphor for dark material coming to consciousness. We "steal" fire (creative power) from the god (the unconscious) and although we become more creative, something has been taken and the god is angry, punishing. We suffer a kind of guilt when new insights are gained. Often, something must be paid back, atoned. Pandora, of course, is part of the story too, part of the punishment meant for mankind. If you get a little fire, you can see more in the dark. You can see the demons, and also the star of hope. Where Prometheus is in the chart may be an indication of where we are going to grab for the fire, the part of the unconscious we want to bring into awareness. Aviator, Wilber Wright who, with his brother, was the first to fly an airplane, had asteroid Prometheus conjunct Mars in Cancer.

2985 Shakespeare was a professional actor and dramatist in London in the late 1500s. His works, their diversity and human insight (not to mention astrological and mythological insights) speak for themselves. Shakespeare produced on average two plays a year for almost twenty years. He was patronized by Queen Elizabeth I and later James I. He was extremely successful and talented in his craft. When this asteroid is conjunct a personal planet or point, acting, playwriting, theater and performance are highlighted, particularly the works of Shakespeare. For example, Lawrence Fishburne, diverse and prolific actor since the age of 12, has asteroid Shakespeare conjunct his North Lunar Node in Leo. He played Othello in Oliver Parker's 1995 film version of Shakespeare's play.

80 Sappho is a tactile, lushes, indulgent and heady asteroid. Her main attribute is the lyre and the gift of poetic expression. A teacher, performer, lyricist and above all, lover, Sappho may express through song, music, fine dinning, lyrics, play, sensual massage, aroma therapy, pleasure and naturally, sex. Aspirations augment, as do creative drive and vitality! The view of the world can become extraordinary and intoxicating when Sappho is activated. If this Asteroid is conjunct or in close aspect to a personal planet or point, something romantic, poetic and creative may express. Consider the sign and house placement for further clues to what might activate this sumptuous body. The poet Elizabeth Barrette Browning had Sappho conjunct Venus in Pisces.

2003VB12 Sedna resides in the icy depths of the Inuit underworld where she rules all marine life, and controls the fate of humans by releasing her bounty to respectful hunters and withholding it from the careless. Sedna is a life/death/life goddess and her recent discovery three times further distant than Pluto may link to the extreme terrain of the unconscious, one where issues of power, authority and respect for life do not separate from a respect for oneself and our planet. The Inuit are animistic, seeing divinity in all things. Sedna may ask us to account for previously unconsidered forms of negligence towards life. An exact placement of Sedna on a personal planet or angle could indicate an affinity with marine life, zoology, marine biology, SCUBA diving, ecology, environmental studies and anything that reinstates a reverence for life on earth, land and sea. Jacques Cousteau, the man who brought the world underneath the waves to life for millions, had Sedna in Aries exactly conjunct the protective and nurturing mother goddess Ceres, trine his Moon in Leo.

4 Vesta, is the goddess of the hearth and worshiped as a virgin, although the original meaning of the word did not imply sexual innocence. A virgin then described a woman who stood on her own, relying on no man for support, identity or companionship. Many of these virgins had lovers and consorts, although they never married or adapted themselves to life with a man. Vesta linked to a personal planet or angle can indicate devotion, religious interest, social welfare, sex as therapy, meditation or sacred initiation. Carl Jung, psychoanalyst noted for his honoring of the sacred feminine, had Vesta conjunct the Sun in Leo in the seventh house. One client with Vesta conjunct the Moon in Cancer in the second house worked as a very highly paid prostitute for over two decades. A therapist with Vesta conjunct the MC in Aquarius ran relationship and tantric sex workshops all over the world.

Asteroid 433 Eros as Passion and Creative Inspiration

Everyone needs to feel the zest of passion, love and creative inspiration from time to time, no matter what their talents and abilities. It is like falling in love, diving into the artisan's pool of magic or reaching out to touch the hem of the ineffable. What planet represents that kind of passion? Eros, the god of love![35]

Just after Valentine's Day 1996, a NEAR satellite left NASA's launch pad on an extended journey to Asteroid 433 Eros, a small body orbiting between Venus and Mars. Its mission: to study the mini-planet's properties and enhance our basic knowledge of the solar system.

This scientific interest in Eros is also reflected in the astrological community's new awareness of asteroids in general. Studying their placement in the chart can add depth and meaning to our path in life. Particular attention now is paid to Eros, the young god of love.

Eros, son of Aphrodite/Venus, is the planet of love, passion, creativity, human sexuality, intimacy and divine union. It has a lot to do with what we get passionate about and how we merge our energies with others to create lasting transformations. Considering Eros in the signs, houses and by aspect will enhance our understanding of desire and fulfillment in everything we do.

The following is a simplified outline of Eros in sign, house and aspect. More information can be obtained by visiting the Internet site: http://www.nrg.com.au/~d- falcon/Eros.htm

Eros in Aries, first house or in aspect to Mars: With this connection, Eros wants action, competition, confrontation and, of course, he wants to win! He can make a game of love and creative pursuits complete with points to score and visiting teams to defeat! The more impossible the objective, the more ardent he becomes. Sometime just by being assertive, the passions awaken.

Eros in Taurus, second house or in aspect to Venus: This pleasure-seeking eye of the bull is ever on the niceties of sensuality. He finds joy in tangible pursuits that revolve around making the body feel good as well as the pleasure of acquisition. Eros here can also become ferociously possessive of those pleasures in an extremely dogmatic way. Being sensual can awaken deeper contact with the soul.

Eros in Gemini, third house or in aspect to Mercury: Curiosity about how things work, why people behave in a certain way, or where some tradition began all contribute to the stimulating mental atmosphere where this Eros likes to live. He uses knowledge as a lure, his mind as bait and his wit as reward. He also might uses these intellectual instruments as a bastion against a cloying emotional world. Stimulate the mind and you awaken the passions!

Eros in Cancer, fourth house or in aspect to the Moon: In this position, Eros experiences a certain measure of affinity and ease. Here the boundaries can dissolve into a space of intimate rapport where the feelings, emotions, fears, pains and ecstasies can mingle into one. Eros does not hesitate at the threshold of creativity now. Once inside, he simply never wants to leave. Nurturing can awaken creativity.

Eros in Leo, fifth house or in aspect to the Sun: Eros here is similar to his fiery counterpart Aries in the desire for action, energy, play and competition. Yet this Eros doesn't just need a playmate; he needs the devotional attention and unfailing love of those who touch his life. Feeling special and creating from the heart brings fulfillment.

Eros in Virgo, sixth house or in aspect to Mercury: Eros here has a lusty and luscious desire nature that shares an affinity with the sign of Taurus. The material elements of life appraise high and that means physical contact, physical nurturing and physical pleasure. Eros here is not afraid to get close and stay close, if the special other or creative project turns out to be *good enough*. Acute analytical endeavors and discrimination can arouse passion and desire.

Eros in Libra, the seventh house and in aspect to Venus: This Eros wants above all to participate with a significant other in many splendid activities. This is the area of personal one-to-one relationships and Eros here has all the longings for the elegance and sophistication that exemplify creative refinement. In this position, life needs to unfold pleasantly and in the company of a beloved other. Passions awaken when least expected!

Eros in Scorpio, the eighth house and in aspect to Pluto: This may be in the place of Eros' greatest affinity. He relates well to the powerful hungers exhibited here, leaving little to modify the creative desires. He does not shun intimacy, physical or otherwise. He is not nervous delving into the unknown or sharing his emotions. This placement must create and transform through merging with others and doing so can bring great fulfillment.

Eros in Sagittarius, the ninth house or in aspect to Jupiter: This placement of Eros needs widespread goals for the future and the space, energy and enthusiasm to live them out. Spontaneous, exuberant, adventurous and fickle, Eros here prefers a lively and challenging creative experience, one that will take him to the limitless corners of the universe. Adventure equals passion!

Eros in Capricorn, in the tenth house or in aspect to Saturn: This position of Eros has powerful concepts about what is good and what is good enough. There is a need for competence and capability that the earthy sign of Taurus would never consider important. Eros here is looking for a type of tangible perfection, or failing that, a certificate of completion at least. The ambition is grand, the heart cautious. Through hard work and challenge, the creative spirit is released.

Eros in Aquarius, in the eleventh house or in aspect to Uranus: This position of Eros carries a high voltage charge with stimulating encounters that need a lot of air space to conduct electromagnetic charms. Eros here desires the weird, the wonderful and the unusual. He thrives on the unexpected and luxuriates in situations that make the more traditional signs squirm with embarrassment. Passions awaken through the pursuit of eccentric goals and zany friends.

Eros in Pisces, the twelfth house or in aspect to Neptune: Here Eros wants to lose all sense of where he ends and another begins. There is desire to return to paradise, drink from the Holy Grail and find union with the divine. He is willing to give up his own identity, allowing it to melt and merge with the beloved (human or creative) until they are no longer distinct but part of a greater whole. Merging, seeking and longing, the creative passions unfold.

146

Part IV

The Daimon as Guiding Spirit: Aspects and Transits as Ally or Adversary

To discover one's daimon or genius is to also find one's weakness, the vulnerable spot of the soul; for a generally recognized characteristic of a god or daimon is jealousy.—Thomas Moore

*H*ow do we discover the deeper levels of our aptitude? What is it in the astrological chart that points to the complexities of our guiding spirit, our daimon, our genius? The aspects do!

Aspects are the degrees of distance existing between planets and points in the chart (with each other) and between natal planets and the transiting (current orbit, progression etc.) positions. These degrees of distance connect the bodies in unique ways, adding depth to the nature of all planets involved. They shade and flavor each other, bringing new insights into otherwise straightforward and unmodified descriptions.

No one position in the horoscope can be read in isolation; it is the patterns of the chart that must be seen and considered as a whole. Only when a natal planet or point is *void of course*, or making no aspect to another position, can it be considered on its own. Often, in that case, it functions out of context with the rest of the chart—a baffling area of life that takes great effort to integrate.

The aspect angles are many, although here will be listed the major ones to consider and a key word meaning for each. It is vital to realize that the connection is what counts, regardless of the angle that links it. A transiting *square* (90 degrees) from Pluto may not manifest much differently from the *trine* (120 degrees), although our orientation to the results might be more accepting with the later. A natal *opposition* (180 degrees) from Saturn may not bring up any more issues than a *sextile* (60 degrees), although the shorter angle may seem easier to resolve. Consider, above all, the connection, and don't be surprised if a conjunction sometimes operates like an opposition, or a quincunx like a square. Be open to any possibility when it comes to aspect degrees.

Glyph	Aspect	Degrees Apart	Meaning
☌	Conjunction	0 to 10	combined power
☍	Opposition	180	objectivity/projection
⊼	Quincunx	150	contrariety/evocation
△	Trine	120	creativity/flow
□	Square	90	adversity/challenge
Q	Quintile	72	talent/progress
✶	Sextile	60	opportunity
∠	Semisquare	45	contention/focus
⌄	Semisextile	30	surprise/adjust
‖	Parallel declination	1	power/union
ⵌ	Parallel declination	180	power/conflict

Other aspects can be used, and suggested reading in the appendix directs the student to references there. The issue of orb is always a lively topic because each astrologer has his or her own favorite limits. Often the conjunction, opposition, square and trine are active within ten degrees, the sextile within six degrees and the lesser aspects around two to four degrees. The parallels are considered tight, within one degree. The best thing to do is to use what works. Ask the question: *Does this person act like they have Saturn square the Moon?* If the answer is *yes,* then the aspect is in orb for them, even if it is thirteen degrees wide. Generally, the closer the orb, the stronger the effect, but curiously, this is not always so. Time and experience will teach the student what degree of orb is

148

authentic to each individual chart.

Aspects and transits are like invitations by the gods, inviting another to join them in a feast, a hunt, a battle or a dance. Some of the gods and goddesses will get along well, feel aligned in their quest and complement each other's goals. Other combinations represent a clash of desires, the need for mediation and adjustment between the two. However they meet, the aim is to find ways to honor the validity of all concerned. After all, they represent bits of ourselves!

It is also important to consider the nature of individuals as *permanent aspects or transits*. The people we are around the most—family, friends, partners, co-workers—will all effect us according to the positions of their own planets. A child's Saturn may be conjunct our Sun, giving us a grounded feeling of responsibility or oppression when we are together. A partner's Pluto can be on our Venus, awakening potent desires and equally potent jealousies and insecurities. The study of this connection between charts is called *synastry* and for those interested in pursuing it further, a reading list is provided in the appendix.

One other note about aspects: *If we don't do them, somebody else will!* Realize that any aspect in the chart, especially ones of intense dichotomy, have a potent desire to live out. If we are uncomfortable with a configuration like Moon square Saturn, we may identify with the Moon by being protective, nurturing and sensitive, and pretend (unconsciously) that we don't have a Saturn at all. Saturn has to go somewhere, and in this case it might be projected onto mother or women friends as a cool, austere and aloof person, or even a harsh, demanding teacher. Or, conversely, we might be self-sufficient, ambitions and removed from our feeling world (Saturn) and find we attract people (especially female) that seem weak, emotive and needy (Moon).

The following information on the aspects and transits are a springboard only. Instead of providing a cookbook list of descriptions, this section is added as a guide to developing a sense of interpretation through pattern combinations. It is offered as a prompt in the understanding of the chart and as a preparation for studying the case history that follows.

Aspects and Transits to Sun

The Sun in the chart portrays a theme, a myth of our purpose and sense of animation. Not necessarily a symbol of innate qualities, the Sun in the chart is something we often must strive towards. It is something to become. In this sense, the Sun is the father in ourselves and often representative of the actual parent as well. Any planet in aspect to the Sun will flavor the sense of purpose, mission and meaning in our life, adding to the myth new and distinct needs and drives. Like the Sun god Apollo, the drive for significance predominates.

Any aspect to the Sun will effect our sense of Self, our power to do and be what we are, and the actualization of our authentic identity. It will color our experience not only of father, but of authority figures and our feeling of strength and power in the world.

Understanding the nature of the planets involved with the Sun by aspect or transit will add meaning and depth. Does the connecting planet bring confidence, energy or charm? Does it add a desire for union or independence? Does it open the floodgates to the underworld or demand that attention be placed on the practicalities of life?

More likely than not, there will be several seemingly conflicting aspects to the Sun, bringing with them desires and goals of diverse natures. The thing to remember is that all the needs, conflicting or not, are valid. To gain the greatest sense of self (Sun) we have to acknowledge and honor whatever is touching it. Transits to this luminary can bring an awakening of Self, a crisis of identity or a combination of the two.

Aspects and Transits to Moon

The Moon in the astrological chart represents the intricate and complex landscape of the feeling realm. It is antithetical to the Sun because it rules the unconscious world of night, primordial feelings and a fundamental need for emotional love and nurturing.

Aspects to the Moon add to and flavor our sense of comfort, security, love and nourishment. They indicate a particular kind of sensitivity to the moods, feelings and undercurrents experienced. An aspect from Mercury might bring sensitivity to thoughts; an aspect from Pluto might make us aware of dark and primordial moods of the group, family or tribe. Saturn might make the Moon contract, protecting through isolation; Neptune might cause it to expand, losing boundaries in search of the divine.

The Moon in the chart has something to do with our image of mother and nurturing as a style of love. Moon connected to Mars might need to fight to feel secure, experiencing a sense of love in the heat of the energy exchange. Moon in aspect to Venus might need to create a feeling of refinement and beauty to feel secure. It might want a sensual and tangible show of nourishment.

Often a strong Moon in the chart (angular house position, in aspect to outer planets, Sun or chart ruler, in the sign of its *rulership* or *exaltation*—Cancer or Pisces) can indicate an aptitude for understanding what the public wants and needs. There is an instinct linked to the collective for better or worse. Transits to this planet can indicate change, movement and awareness in the areas of emotional security, nurturing, home and family.

Aspects and Transits to Mercury

Mercury symbolizes the myriad aspects of comprehension and elucidation that help bring creative concepts to life. It is no mistake that the ancients made Mercury the god of travel, protector of the roads. This god leads us through the familiar and not so familiar terrain with the aim of discovering new meaning and new significance between the two. As god of the crossroads, he is the god of choice, the one who points out the path to follow. A sound relationship with this aspect of the self is vital for fulfilling our vocation in life.

Mercury rules communication, travel, thinking, teaching and learning. It is the signification of conscious thought, perception and categorization. Mercury is an index not so much to intelligence, but to curiosity, theorizing, and perception. It is the part of the intellect that can make a relationship between what is known and what is yet to be discovered. It is the bridge we build to understand the unfamiliar.

Mercury was called Hermes by the Ancient Greeks and was born form the adulterous union of Zeus and Maia. He was unique in that, of all the offspring of Zeus, his jealous wife Hera did not hate him. Some even had it that she suckled him herself, an unheard of act of acceptance towards Zeus's product of infidelity.

Aspects to Mercury flavor the way we think, communicate and move about. Mars may make it snappy, feisty; Pluto may give a sense of depth and concealment. Neptune may bring a world of fantasy into play; connections to the Sun can mean we become ourselves by *doing* Mercury. A transit to Mercury awakens the needs of this planet and can manifest as changes, choices and opportunities to *move,* in any sense of the word.

Aspects and Transits to Venus

The traditional view of Venus in the astrological chart portrays this planet as a symbol for the powers of attraction. Venus rules love, affection, beauty and what we value aesthetically and artistically. Where Venus resides is where we can attract, cajole and charm others, where we can win them over to our side. It also depicts a desire for relatedness, not so much for the sake of merging but for the determination of deeper values. Through one-to-one relationships, personal values are identified, refined and adopted.

Aspects touching Venus will alter, enhance and modify what it is we attract, how we determine if something is beautiful and who we go about relating to. An aspect from Uranus may give us eccentric or rebellious tastes, as well as split us down the middle with the twin desires of freedom and closeness. An aspect to Saturn may ground us with a serious sense of responsibility, making our artistic expression hard work. Or it could make us feel isolated and unfulfilled in relationship, until we find creative ways of expressing the Saturn side. The split could be between luxuriant pleasure and disciplined focus.

Transits, especially from outer planets, can strongly affect our sense of values. They can signify a time when what we think we want is not that at all, and new goals and desires must be invented if we are to feel fulfilled.

Aspects and Transits to Mars

Traditionally, Mars (or the Greek Ares) was the god of war. He arose from a primitive vegetation god and developed first into Ares, brutal, blood-thirsty, battle-crazed and not terribly successful. He then progressed into the Roman Mars, who was somewhat

152

more refined, having the qualities of strategy and honor as well as barbarian vigor. Mars was a lot more popular than Ares, who was shunned by gods and mortals alike.

Although the savage nature of Ares/Mars was disdained, the Greeks did not mind calling him forth when they needed his interminable courage, and neither should we! Mars is what gets us moving! It gives us a sense of healthy aggression, the *no* that keeps us from being abused and the *yes* that dares to apply for the job, submit the paper, take the necessary risk. When we feel weak, downtrodden or feeble, it is Mars in the chart we must look to and honor by finding healthy ways to express our unique assertive nature.

Aspects to Mars will effect our raw and vital healthy aggression. The Sun can make it shine though everything we do (think of Aries here), the Moon may make us more cautious, mulling things over before we take a stand. Jupiter can give so much extra enthusiasm that we aren't happy unless we are in command, king of the hill. Saturn can contain the energy, using it creatively in steady measure, step by step by step. Think about what the contacting planet wants and needs and then consider how that might sit with the needs of Mars. Do they get along? Is there compatibility? Is there incongruity? What are they saying to each other?

Transits to Mars will work in a similar manner. Mars is being awakened, and its ability to go forth in the world and initiate, assert and contest in the style that he is adorned (sign and house position) will determine our level of vitality and zest for life.

Aspects and Transits to Jupiter

The Roman Jupiter, or Greek Zeus, was king of the gods on Mt. Olympus. He gained the position by tricking his father Kronos (Saturn) into drinking a potion that would make him ill. Kronos had been swallowing his offspring whole in the fear that one would some day supplant him, although Rhea, Zeus's mother, had fed Kronos a swaddled rock instead of the infant Zeus when he was born. She hoped that her young son might avoid the fate of his siblings. On maturity, Zeus, in disguise, offered his father the poisoned cup, and soon the offspring of Kronos, and the rock, disgorged. Zeus vanquished Kronos and the reign of the Olympians began.

Zeus bestowed sovereignty over various realms to his brothers. The underworld went to Hades (Pluto) and the oceans and islands to Poseidon (Neptune). His sisters, Hestia, Hera and Demeter, gained rule over the cycles of life—marriage, childbirth and the control of the seasons and crops.

Traditionally, Jupiter/Zeus is the archetype of creativity, vision and enthusiastic expansion. Jupiter reaches goals by eagerly flashing its robust and confident power about, often going overboard in the process. Jupiter finds meaning and purpose in the otherwise mundane, creating myth out of daily routine. It is a fair distance from the Sun, from the authentic identity, seeking greater significance and influence in the outer world with the benefit of a distant perspective.

Jupiter's powers of procreation were notorious, fathering hundreds of offspring with goddesses and mortal women alike. He is a symbol for abundance, creativity and power. Any planet in aspect to this god is going to get a taste of his vision.

Consider the contrast between the sensual Venus in contact with Jupiter as opposed to Mars. With Venus, relationships expand, values and a sense of beauty develop as far and wide as possible and amorous adventures may be pursued. Mars is going to want to expand in other ways, widening its authority and expressing its will and initiative. Mercury in aspect might have very big ideas or study multiple cultures, belief systems or languages. Saturn might argue with Jupiter about the difference between vision and practicality. The more we understand what each individual planet wants and has to offer, the more we can intuit what they will do when combined in aspect pattern.

Transits to natal Jupiter bring the urge to expand, believe and create. The more freedom we have to experience these urges and express them creatively, the more fulfilled we feel.

Aspects and Transits to Saturn

Saturn is the traditional antithesis of Jupiter. Where Jupiter expands, Saturn contracts. Where Jupiter optimistically sees hope, Saturn pessimistically sees disheartenment. Where Jupiter has only fiery vision, Saturn embodies concrete reality. Yet Saturn is the form, function and gravity that keeps life on earth from floating off into the cosmos. Without Saturn, there is no physical existence. Although with it, that physical existence will always be imperfect, flawed.

Saturn, or Kronos, was born a Titan from the union of Uranus and Gaea. Because Uranus found his offspring repulsive, he shoved them back into the bowels of the earth as they emerged. Upset, Gaea plotted against Uranus beseeching her children to aid her plan. None would, except Kronos, who took the scythe his mother offered and in the still of the night sliced off his father's genitals and cast them into the sea. From the drops of black blood that fell to the earth sprang the Furies, goddesses of retribution, a few monstrous giants and the Ash Tree Nymphs. From the foaming scraps in the sea arose the wondrous goddess of love, Aphrodite. Kronos then freed his siblings and set himself up as king of the gods.

From the very beginning of his rule, Saturn felt fear and distrust. He was joined with his sister Rhea, yet he so dreaded the potential power of his offspring he swallowed them whole as they were born. Rhea was not happy, and we already know what happened next: Jupiter repeats history and dethrones his father, bringing to life Saturn's worst fear.

It is interesting, in light of the mythology, how often those with strong Saturn placements experience the climb to and subsequent fall from a place of towering triumph and authority. Here Saturn symbolizes the intrinsic need for recognition, respect and supremacy that sits side by side with overwhelming fear and insecurity. Fear of success. Fear of failure. Both must be faced with strongly placed Saturn aspects (particularly Sun, Moon and angles).

Saturn can represent an inner pain and apprehension residing deep within the individual. The sign, house and aspect position delineates the nature of that apprehension. They also describe the power that may face the fears and turn the painful flaws to fortune.

Think of the planets that aspect Saturn as allies to the cause. There is something about each one of them that may add, assist and support us in facing the shadowed side of ourselves. Jupiter brings optimism, the Moon can offer empathy and sensitivity. Mars gives courage, the Sun can bring honor. Not all aspects to Saturn will be simple to understand—the deep and complex nature of Saturn-Pluto needs very careful handling to enhance our power in the world without becoming a despot, large or small—yet each will have something to offer and a desire to be expressed.

Transits to Saturn give us insight into our healthy ambition. They ask us to examine how far up the ladder we have climbed. It asks if we have we missed any steps along the way. It asks us to consider deeply if our current path is still valid. It checks in on our relationships to appraise their validity. Saturn's questions are neither light nor frivolous, yet honest answers can bring us closer to authentic fulfillment than we can often imagine. This is its promise, the Golden Age.

Aspects and Transits to Chiron

In myth and in life, Chiron is about suffering in the face of despair, random factors where there seems no solution. It is about the inexplicable fate of offering only good and receiving only treachery. It is remarkable that Chiron never grew bitter and vengeful, as would seemingly be his right.

Chiron embodies the archetype of the *wounded healer*. He is the outcast who passes his wealth of knowledge on through the arts of healing, philosophy, astrology, music, strategy and war tactics. He was incurable, mortally wounded yet unable to die because of his immortality. In this way, he suffered deeply until at last he was released from his pain by trading places in the underworld with the Titan, Prometheus.

Illegitimate son of Saturn, Chiron also is the *random factor* in life that, like his sudden release through the exchange with Prometheus, indicates a complete and unequivocal alteration of events. We think we are headed in one direction and then, without warning, we are on a completely new path. In this sense, Chiron is as unpredictable as the sky god Uranus.

Chiron is about building bridges of knowledge, understanding and compassion and any planet connected to it is going to be part of this cause. Mercury may bring expression of these ideas through the written or spoken word. The Moon or Neptune may find Chiron working with the weak, sick or wounded in hospitals or institutions. The Sun may make a career out of Chiron associated motifs: healing, therapies, astrology, the occult, martial arts, herbal medicine, acupuncture, divination. Venus may simply fall in love with a person of this ilk. Transits to Chiron will awaken this side of the self and how he is placed in the natal chart by sign, house and aspect, will shed light on the results.

Aspects and Transits to Uranus

Traditionally, Uranus is a symbol of pure, unadulterated mental intellect. It is also called *Sky*, *Starry Sky* or *Starry Heaven* and rules the cool and orderly realm of perception, consciousness and rational thought. The original god of the heavens, Uranus is not concerned with the base and earthy life, the imperfections of fallible beings or the raw desires of nature. Paradoxically, those things most repulsive to him are precisely what he creates in his offspring with Gaea.

Uranus, or Ouranos, was born without union from Gaea/Earth. As the personification of the sky, he is first ruler of the universe and mate of Gaea. He populates the earth with the first born races, the Hecatonchires, the Cyclopes and the twelve Titans. His creations give him quite a shock.

The Hecatonchires are hideous giants with great might and size, each having one hundred hands and fifty heads. They offended and appalled the pure intellect of Uranus and, repulsed, he hid them away in a secret place of the earth as soon as each one was born.

When Gaea gave birth the race of Titans, she was starting to get very annoyed. She could not forget the fate of her other offspring and, as noted in the discussion of Saturn, she convinced Kronos, her youngest son, to displace him. He and the other Titans, all except Oceanus, agreed as Kronos lopped off the genitals of Uranus and tossed them into the sea.

This horrific insurrection produced the sisters of retribution, giants, nymphs and the ravishing Aphrodite. It is important to note that the strife inherent in Saturn and Uranus can result in a variety of spawn, the least of them the goddess of beauty and love.

Anything contacting Uranus will be electrified! It adds zest, audacity, energy and a restless urge for freedom. It also adds a potent measure of will power. Not every planet in the chart is going to like it.

Consider the difference between a Moon-Uranus contact and a Sun-Uranus one. Which planet combination will feel more at home, easier to live out in unison? What about a combination of Mars and Uranus? Does it give more self-will, autonomy and direction, or less? What about Mercury and Uranus? Would that quicken the thoughts? Take them to extraordinary landscapes? Make for extreme restlessness perhaps?

Transits to Uranus tend to jolt us out of the status quo. If we have been in a job that is boring, a relationship that is long dried up or associating with a circle of friends that seem like zombies, transits to Uranus can be the lightening bolt that strikes, sending us tumbling towards a whole new path in life.

Aspects and Transits to Neptune

The astrological Neptune portrays a myriad of meanings from the dreamy depths of the watery unconscious, the longings of spiritual aspirations, the obsession of powerful desires to the revelation of the divine beloved. Some say it is where we seek the ineffable, or where, conversely, the ineffable seeks us. Whatever it is, this god of the oceans, waters and seas, brother to Jupiter and lover of Demeter, can be confusing!

Neptune can symbolize a place of confusion and deception because it represents something too intangible for the mundane world to decipher. Certainly, Neptune's complex meaning defies summing up in a list of key words. It would be easier to show Neptune through literature—perhaps in the image of Sir Arthur Conrad Doyle's *Sherlock Holmes* or in Milton's *Paradise Lost*—or perhaps Neptune could be expressed though dance, theater or the fine arts. Neptune is something that must be felt and experienced rather than explained.

A deeper understanding of Neptune can come from a personal taste of despair that goes with a separation from the god. Many paths, including alcohol, addiction, obsession, desire, love, devotion, creativity, manipulation, dreams, fantasy, madness and dissolving boundaries are followed in the search for the illusive redeemer. All these things swirl around the archetype of Neptune, yet any planet connected to Neptune by aspect is understood when the same primary questions are asked. What do you need? What do you want? What do you have to offer? How do you get along?

Neptune may enjoy the contact with Mercury in a water sign,

adding articulation, musical ability and poetic expression to the creative side of the planets. Yet how would Mars in a fire sign fair by aspect to the god of the seas? Would there be confusion around the way he asserted his will? Would there be a conflict between severity and compassion: between *yes* and *no*?

Transits to Neptune are felt according to the natal aspect links to personal planets and points. This can be a time of change, initiated by a sense of immersion, disillusionment and inner inspiration. Again, all we can ask is *what is it that you want?* With Neptune, there sometimes is no immediate answer.

Aspects and Transits to Pluto

Pluto, or Hades, is the god of death. He ruled the underworld allotted him after the abscission of his father, Saturn. At first he reigned alone, then later with his queen, Persephone. A cloistered deity, Pluto rarely encountered others unless they went down to meet him. When his need was desperate, he erupted from the depths of the underworld to seek fulfillment of his desires.

In astrological terms, Pluto also rules death and its inevitable retinue: mourning, transformation, change and letting go. This planet is associated with the immense pain and suffering that corresponds to great loss. It can relate to the breaking down of a facade or strongly held identity, the physical loss of someone dear or the loss of a familiar way of life, and there may be vehemence attached to it. Pluto in this capacity is associated with rage and violence.

The anger goes deeper than not having our needs met. Perhaps it is associated with the impotence we feel against the greater necessity of life. Pluto is associated with fate and in this capacity neither mere mortals nor the mightiest gods have any authority.

Pluto also is the god of hidden treasures. Although planets in aspect to Pluto can expect to take periodic journeys into the depths of the underworld, they also have the opportunity to return to the land of the living with a bounty of wealth. This may be spiritual, psychological, intellectual or literal, all according to the nature of the planets concerned. Mercury may plumb the depths of the deeper self, experience mental anxiety, paranoia and agitation, although eventually it may come through the experience with greater levels of comprehension, intellect and cognition. Those with Venus in aspect to Pluto may meet their fate through relationships, yet return from the underworld with emotional freedom and a new and more authentic sense of love. Saturn facing Pluto may have to deal with awesome issues of power and control, primitive urges vs. civilized aspirations, yet eventually may learn to become its own authority. Contacts to Pluto push us to the edge. What we do when we get there is free will.

Aspects and Transits to the Lunar Nodes

"If we fail to nourish our souls, they wither, and without soul, life ceases to have meaning. The creative process shrivels in the absence of continual dialogue with the soul. And creativity is what makes life worth living. Marion Woodman

Aspects and transits to the Lunar Nodes, both North and South, can pertain to people that we attract, and these people usually have something to offer when it comes to personal growth, distinction, aptitude and fulfillment. For example, an activated South Node can coincide with the appearance of a person from the past. They reemerge without warning, often requiring some assistance or help. A transit to the South Node suggests that the experiences related to the sign and house the Node falls in will be amplified, hard to miss. These contacts can seem as if someone else needs all the guidance, however, the individual experiencing the transit often grows from the encounters.

Because the South Node indicates the familiar, transits or aspects here can become a mask or defense against exploring any new territory, inner or outer. A planet conjunct the South Node can indicate a need to rebuild a new and creative quality relating to what that planet represents. It's not always easy or comfortable to answer this call. If the South Node represents things already experienced, already gathered, it may be important to use the positive aspects of the sign, house and planets associated with the North Node to further explore new and unfamiliar experiences.

Remember, whatever transits the South Node will awaken the North Node as well. Transits to the North Node can bring new people and experiences into the life, situations that can require deliberate choices and decisive action. This is the unexplored territory that beckons us toward the future. It can be rewarding to follow, although something from the past, a belief, friends, familiarity, must be let go of. The urge, at times, may be to run back into the South Node and forsake any growth, at least for the time being. This is the natural polarity of these two points and it is at times "one step forward, two steps back," or visa versa. The more consciousness placed on the goals for the future the more unconscious the past becomes, and an unconscious past is something to be reckoned with. The paradox is, we meet it face on as it projects out into our lives!

By acknowledging both where the future lies and the origins we come from, a more symmetrical relationship can be made between the Nodes, so one is not forsaken for the other. The polarity of the signs and houses in which the Nodes are placed is vital to understand. When activated by transit, this understanding becomes vivid, often dramatized in our day to day life.

Part V

Standing at the Crossroads and Making the Apt Choice: Example Charts

Visionary power
Attends the motions of the viewless winds
Embodied in the mystery of words.—William Wordsworth

Several example charts are offered to show how all the considerations may be put together to form a feeling for direction and a sense, if not a list, of the aptitudes and talents at our disposal. The more we work with an array of charts, experimenting with known people, friends, clients and family members, the greater our own skill will be in answering this most important question: *What is it I am meant to be doing?*

Example One, Hedy Lamarr

The following chart is of an extraordinary woman born in Austria prior to World War I. She is famous as a Hollywood leading lady playing opposite actors such as Spencer Tracy and Clark Gable (one of her six husbands), and also infamous for her earlier role in a steamy Czechoslovakian film called *Ecstasy*, released in 1933, in which she was filmed in the nude—a first worldwide for the industry and quite controversial. The film was banned in the United States and the United Kingdom for many years.

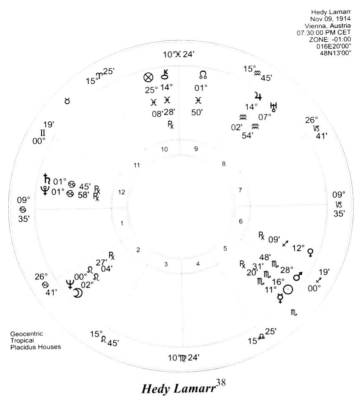

Hedy Lamarr
Nov 09, 1914
Vienna, Austria
07:30:00 PM CET
ZONE: -01:00
016E20'00"
48N13'00"

10°♓24'

15°♈25'

⊗ ⚷
25° 14°

♓ ♓
08'28' 50'
℞

♋
01°

15°♒45'

♃
14° ♅
♒ 07'
02' ♒
54'

26°
♑
41'

♉

19'
00°
♓

ℏ 01° ♋ 45' ℞
♆ 01° ♋ 58' ℞
09°
♋
35'

12

11

10   9

8

7

6

09°
♑
35'

℞ 09°
48' ♐ 12° ♀
♌ 27' ℞
04'
00° ♌
♇ 02'
☽
26°
♋
41'

2

3   4

5

℞ ♏
20'31' ♏ 28° ♂
♏ 16° 19'
11° ☉ 00°
☿

♏

Geocentric
Tropical
Placidus Houses

15°♌45'

15°♎25'

10°♍24'

Hedy Lamarr[38]

Hedy's notoriety does not stop on the silver screen. This woman also held the patent for an invention that revolutionized the use of radio waves: a technique now called spread-spectrum broadcasting.

What talents, aptitudes and resources propelled Hedy through her life? What deep inner needs where fulfilled by the paths she chose? Although hindsight tends to be crystal clear, examining her chart and matching it against the exceptional experiences she had can aid in our understanding of the horoscope as a map of aptitude and direction.

The first area to note in Hedy's chart is the grouping of planets in Scorpio in the fifth house—Sun conjunct Mercury, square Uranus/Jupiter in Aquarius and trine the Ascendant, which indicates a need for depth. There is a sensitivity for the darker undercurrents in

164

the collective (especially with Saturn conjunct Pluto in the twelfth house), a certain glamour and desire to shock, an ability to perceive in unconventional ways and a genuine need for erotic expression. All of this is focused in the fifth house of creative self-expression.

It is no surprise that Hedy had the charisma to attract the attention of the film industry when she was still in her teens. It is also no surprise that she would gain a sense of self (Sun) from performing in an artistic yet erotic (Scorpio in the fifth house) way. Her nude scene rocked the world. At the time of filming, she was 18.

Hedy was married and divorced six times. Although her relationship life will not be explored here in depth, the student is free to consider the implications of her chart against her emotional life. Her first marriage marked, however, a pivotal point in her career.

Hedy's first marriage was to Fritz Mandl, an older man, an arms manufacturer/supplier and Nazi sympathizer. He was possessive of the young Hedy and kept her close by his side during his arms discussions and transfers—perhaps more as a trophy than a wife.

She learned a great deal about the weapons industry from the meetings held behind closed doors in her home. She also developed a fear and loathing of the Nazis. (Consider Saturn, ruler of her seventh house husband conjunct Pluto in Cancer in the twelfth house trine Mercury in Scorpio.)

She felt oppressed and imprisoned by her husband and in 1937, she slipped the maid who guarded her a sedative and ran away to London. There she met studio chief Louis B. Mayer who signed her to MGM. Her next move was straight to Hollywood.

Hedy's ability to enchant on the silver screen can be attributed to the Moon (chart ruler) conjunct Neptune (Midheaven ruler) in the second house of talents and resources. Her allure itself was a talent in this case that brought her a hefty income as a means of support and a lot of tenth house notoriety. This ability is underscored not only by the already mentioned fifth house activity but also by the Sun/Venus midpoint (artistic flare, charisma and seductiveness) exactly conjunct Mars in Scorpio, again in the fifth house of creative self-expression. Her look was copied by actresses and moviegoers alike as she inspired the center-parted hairstyle popular with women throughout the 1940s. Her trendsetting Venus in Sagittarius square the Midheaven and quincunx the Ascendant may be in play here as is the fashion setting Neptune-Moon.

Yet, Hedy was not just a film star of the '30s and '40s and '50s. She was also an inventor who patented an idea for *frequency hopping*, a form of wireless data networking.

Hedy felt great fear, sensitivity and social concern for the rise of Nazi power in Europe. (Consider the grand trine in *water* including Chiron conjunct the Midheaven in Pisces, Ascendant in Cancer and Sun-Mercury in Scorpio.) At a dinner party in early 1940, she teamed up with the wildly eccentric composer George Antheil and together they developed her idea for a *Secret Communications System*.[36] What better example of Sun-Mercury in Scorpio square Jupiter/Uranus in Aquarius in the eighth? They received a patent for the device in 1942, and although is was not used as she intended (to free radio controlled torpedoes from signal jamming), it is now used in cellular phones, wireless internet, traffic signals and defense satellites.

It may have been her paranoia and fear (Saturn in the twelfth conjunct Pluto-Ascendant) that pushed her to develop the concept of the advanced technology (Jupiter-Uranus in Aquarius in the eighth). It is all speculation now because she died January 19, 2000, leaving only interviews and an autobiography published in the '60s (she sued the publishing house regarding alleged inaccuracies) to attest to her motivations. She did say of her career in the film industry, *"I did what I did for love."* This exemplifies her Pisces Chiron-Midheaven- North Node trine the Cancer Ascendant.

On March 11, 1977, when transiting Uranus was hovering between ten and eleven degrees of Scorpio conjunct her Mercury and trine the Ascendant and Midheaven, Hedy received honor and acknowledgement form the *Electronic Frontier Foundation* when they awarded her their *Pioneer Award* for her invention of spread-spectrum broadcasting. She was 84 years old and the award was accepted by one of her three children, Anthony Loder. He said of her, *"She's been forgotten. But she contributes so much to an older generation. A lot of men fell in love with her . And now the younger generation is benefiting from the unknown creative work that she did."*[37]

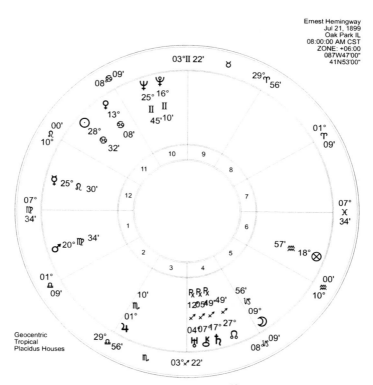

Ernest Hemingway
Jul 21, 1899
Oak Park IL
08:00:00 AM CST
ZONE: +06:00
087W47'00"
41N53'00"

Ernest Hemingway[42]

Example Two, Ernest Hemingway

The second example chart, Ernest Hemingway, is offered for three reasons. First, he was an exceptional man with an aptitude for writing that he recognized early in his youth and spent his life perfecting. Second, there is a plethora of information about this man, enabling the student to study the chart further and from many perspectives. Third, as an author, his chart exemplifies how the division between the reality of the authentic life and the characters one creates is nonexistent. It shows that characteristics acted in a play, portrayed on the screen or written in a novel can be as valid an expression of the self as any of the natural traits exhibited in daily life.

Hemingway was the son of a physician father and a mother who was a music teacher and artist. His early school interests included science, hunting and fishing, yet by the time he graduated from

167

high school, he had begun his career as a writer, working for the *Kansas City Star.* In 1918, he volunteered for the Red Cross as an ambulance driver and was injured (reportedly the first American shot on the Italian front). He fell in love with his nurse while recovering, germinating the inspiration for *Farewell to Arms.*

Returning to the states after being rejected by the nurse (several years his senior), he married his first of five wives and moved to Paris to write. He was influenced and tutored by Ezra Pound, Gertrude Steinem and F. Scott Fitzgerald (when the older man was sober) and started developing his unique writing style. Unfortunately, in 1922, his wife lost a suitcase on a train trip; it was filled with his collection of unpublished works. There was nothing for him to do but start over.

Hemingway's notoriety grew once he began publishing, and his friends were often agitated by his works, finding themselves portrayed with little or thin disguise. His parents did not approve of most of the subject matter or its handling, particularly his mother who felt he had lost his honor and nobility. There were many angry exchanges between mother and son on this topic.

In spite of, or perhaps because of, his potent ties with his mother and the early loss of his father who committed suicide during Hemingway's first Saturn return, he developed an extremely *macho* edge. He was the unabashed alpha male, hunting game in Africa, having affairs, dominating situations and going to war.

Hemingway's editor said that there where three pieces to the puzzle of Hemingway: The man that really lived, the writer and the celebrity. He felt that no one, including Hemingway, could see a clear division between the boundaries. After many great literary achievements, five marriages and three children and after his father before him (who shot himself with a pistol during a long term of depression), Ernest Hemingway blew off his own head with a shotgun at age sixty-two. It was a brutal end to an extraordinary life.

The first place to note this man's talents and aptitudes is an investigation of his chart ruler (and Midheaven ruler), Mercury in Leo in the twelfth. It is interesting how much Hemingway worked *behind the scenes,* not just in the creation of his fiction but in his work as war correspondence and investigative reporter. He sought the secret facts behind the veil of enemy territory, an apt example of Mercury's placement and of the aspect to Neptune in the tenth house.

With Gemini ruling the tenth house and Pluto-Neptune-South Node there, the feeling was that he must report, teach or tell of situations on the edge that stretch the imagination and sense of fate. The North Node particularly suggests a need not just to list facts but to balance them with meaning and purpose. The opposition to the fourth house Sagittarius planets evokes a tight rope walk between what he knew and what he believed to be true.

His T-Square with Mars in Virgo in the first house pulls the god of war in with the god of death (Pluto) and the god of form, function and fear (Saturn). Unlike Hedy Lamarr's chart, where Saturn and Pluto are conjunct in the twelfth house, Hemingway has them in opposition in the tenth and fourth. We can conjecture here about his experience of his parents and women in general, for this configuration effects strongly his sense of the feminine.[39] What is particularly interesting in terms of talents and resources, however, is the focus on Mars in Virgo.

Hemingway was first and foremost a list maker. He never initiated (Mars) anything without first going through a ritual of itemizing, categorizing, pricing and analyzing. He has left behind, seemingly, more lists of things than pages of literary works. The strong Virgo element is in evidence here, as is the Mars that boils under the pressure cooker of the Saturn-Pluto squares. No wonder he pushed forth a macho facade. The tension on Mars obligated him to express it, lest he explode.

What made Hemingway a great writer? The secret may be more in the mystery of life than in the chart. However, there are clues as to why he wrote.

When Mercury is not in the same sign as the Sun (it can only be in the sign of, the sign before or the sign after) it is less easy for the individual to express his or her essential self. Being who we are (Sun) is not so easy to communicate (Mercury) because the planets are in different signs and have different orientations to life.

In Hemingway's chart, Mercury is in Leo and in the twelfth house, not an overly forthcoming domain. Just like Mars in Virgo feels the need to overly accentuate assertive male qualities because there is a *doubt*, this Mercury, which feels the pressure of being chart ruler and Midheaven ruler, needs to express the self in dramatic ways. It wants to expose secrets, reveal the hidden meaning and touch the collective heart, all with a unique artistic style and flare. Of course, wanting to do a thing and doing it are not always the same, but in the case of Hemingway, it was.

That he became a mouthpiece for the feelings and emotions of the collective conscious and unconscious (Sun in Cancer in the eleventh and Mercury in Leo in the twelfth) is evident. That he did it through the use of the written word is not a surprise, especially with Sun square Jupiter in the third house of communication. That he traveled the world, often finding himself in strange, war torn and exotic lands in his occupation is also no surprise (Uranus, ruler of the day-to-day sixth house opposite the Midheaven and square the Ascendant, along with the emphasis of Sagittarius in the fourth house, especially the North Node, and Jupiter square the Sun).

He often wrote material ahead of its time, as in his 1922 story, *Up in Michigan,* which is basically about date rape. This was not a subject open for discussion, although Hemingway's strong Uranus propelled him toward the controversial material, not unlike Hedy Lamarr's progressive Uranian influence propelled her toward invention and daring.

What made Hemingway a great writer? Impossible to answer. He did say, however, that *"The most essential gift for a good writer is a built-in, shock-proof, shit detector. This is the writer's radar and all great writers have had it."*[40] Perhaps this mechanism that was so strongly in play throughout Hemingway's career is symbolized by his Saturn in Sagittarius in the fourth house trine Mercury in Leo in the twelfth house. A *shit detector* if there ever was one and no doubt an inheritance from his father.

It is also instructive and fascinating to look at Hemingway's chart in terms of the characters he created. Consider the opposition between Neptune in Gemini and Saturn in Sagittarius. The story that won him the Noble prize for literature in 1953, *The Old Man and the Sea,* is a story about an old, lonely fisherman named Santiago who battles with the sea, catches the greatest marlin he has ever seen and loses the entire carcass to sharks on the long journey back to land. As pointed out succinctly by Dennis Elwell *"...when he returns to land exhausted he has nothing to show except its awesome skeleton. That fishes bones are a vivid Saturn-Neptune image.*[41] Much of what Hemingway wrote was the flesh and blood of his own soul as portrayed by the turbulent opposition between outer planets in the fourth and tenth.

The student may wish to explore this chart further, matching transits and progressions to the abundant information on this man's life. As an example, note transiting Jupiter conjunct the Midheaven and passing through the tenth house in 1953, when Hemingway was awarded the Nobel Prize. The planet of recognition and expansion had hit the highest elevation in the chart, an acknowledgement of his achievements in the world. Contrast that with his battle with depression and subsequent suicide when Pluto was hovering over his Ascendant in Virgo and Saturn transiting his Sun by opposition.

* * *

The best way to become familiar with identifying planetary indications of talent and aptitude is to study the charts of many people. The important thing is to have an open mind and keep personal biases and judgments out of the picture. The object here is to understand and communicate how we best can become who we are! The possibilities of the symbols are endless, although sometimes that one consultation, one opening thought or idea, is enough to give another person the confidence to knock on a new door of destiny. The choice of what to do when it opens, of course, is always a matter of free will.

Appendix

Glossary of Terms and Symbols

Aries ♈
Taurus ♉
Gemini ♊
Cancer ♋
Leo ♌
Virgo ♍

Libra ♎
Scorpio ♏
Sagittarius ♐
Capricorn ♑
Aquarius ♒
Pisces ♓

Sun ☉
Moon ☽
Mercury ☿
Venus ♀
Mars ♂
Jupiter ♃
Saturn ♄
Uranus ♅
Neptune ♆
Pluto ♇

North Node ☊
South Node ☋
Chiron ⚷
Vesta ⚶
Ceres ?
Pallas ⚴
Juno ⚵
Eros
Fortuna ⊗

☌ Conjunction—0 to 10 degrees apart
☍ Opposition—180 degrees apart
⚻ Quincunx—150 degrees apart
△ Trine—120 degrees apart
□ Square—90 degrees apart
Q Quintile—75 degrees apart
⚹ Sextile—60 degrees apart
∠ Semisquare—45 degrees apart
⚺ Semisextile—30 degrees apart
‖ Parallel—1 degree of declination
⫴ Contraparallel—1 degree of declination

Cardinal Fire—♈
Cardinal Earth—♑

Cardinal Air—♎
Cardinal Water—♋
Fixed Fire—♌
Fixed Earth—♉
Fixed Air—♒
Fixed Water—♏
Mutable Fire—♐
Mutable Earth—♍
Mutable Air—♊
Mutable Water—♓

Air Signs—The three signs of the zodiac in the element of air: Gemini, Libra and Aquarius.

Alchemy—Medieval chemical science. The symbolism of the alchemical process can be seen as a metaphor for processes in the unconscious and the path of individuation.

Ananke—The Greek goddess of Fate. Also known as Necessity.

Angular Houses—Those houses that correspond to the four angles: first, fourth, seventh and tenth.

Aphrodite—The Greek goddess of love.

Apollo—The Greek god of light, music and prophesy, son of Zeus.

Applying—A planet that is moving towards an exact aspect to a slower moving planet or point.

Aptitude—Inclination, natural ability, talent or tendency. From middle English *aptitudo/* fitness.

Archetype—An underlying theme or motif that occurs in all places, in all cultures, in all times as recognizable images, i.e. the Fool, the Wise Old Man, the Virgin, marriage, death, love etc. They emerge from the collective unconscious and appear in legends, dreams, fairy tales, myths, religions, literature, art and films.

Ares— The Greek god of war. He is similar but not identical to the Roman god Mars, who tends to be equally assertive but less raw, clumsy and bloodthirsty.

Artemis—The Greek goddess of moon, twin sister of Apollo.

Athene—(1) Greek goddess of wisdom, strategy, arts and crafts. Also known as Pallas Athene, counterpart to the Roman Minerva. (2) Asteroid 2 Pallas Athene, orbiting between Mars and Jupiter.

Ascendant—Also called the rising sign, the point where the eastern horizon and the ecliptic intersect.

Aspect—The angular connection between two planets or points in the 360 degrees of the astrological chart.

Asteroid—A minor planet in orbit around the Sun. Most are found in the "asteroid belt" between Mars and Jupiter. The earth crossing asteroids orbit between Venus and Mars, crossing the orbit of earth.

Atropos—One of the three Greek sisters of Fate. Atropos cuts the thread ending the measure of life.

Cadent Houses—Those houses that fall third from each angular house: the third, sixth, ninth and twelfth.

Cardinal Signs—Those signs of the zodiac associated with the angular houses, Aries, Cancer, Libra and Capricorn.

Castor—The immortal twin of Pollux in the constellation of Gemini.

Ceres—(1) The daughter of Kronos and sister to Zeus, also known as Demeter (Greek). She is an image of divine mother, goddess of the earth portrayed with a daughter but no husband or consort. (2) Asteroid 1 Ceres, the first asteroid to be discovered. Orbits between Mars and Jupiter.

Chiron—(1) Son of Saturn. A Greek Centaur whose wisdom was renown. He was mortally wounded but could not die, symbolizing the archetype of the wounded healer. (2) Also, a comet like mini-planet orbiting the Sun between Saturn and Uranus discovered in 1977.

Clotho—One of the three Greek sisters of Fate. Clotho spins the thread that represents mortal life.

Collective Conscious—Psychic contents that is common and conscious to many individuals.

Collective Unconscious—Common psychic contents that links many individuals yet remains unconscious.

Complex—A theme or idea that carries a strong emotion charge. At the core of the complex resides an archetype or mythic theme.

Consciousness—What we think we are aware of.

Kronos—The Greek father of Zeus, counterpart of the Roman Saturn.

Cusp—The boundary (first and last degree) between two astrological houses or the boundary between signs as shown by the last degree (29) or the first degree (0).

Daimon—An archetype of power, divinity, ineffability and fate. Our guiding spirit or genius.

Descendant—The point opposite the Ascendant or rising sign.

Demeter—Mother of Persephone, goddess of the harvest and counterpart to the Roman Ceres.

Dionysos—Greek god of ecstasy and divine madness.

Derivative Houses—The method assigns meanings to each astrological house relative to it becoming the first house, i.e., the eighth house indicates the financial resources of the partner because it is the second house (resources) from the seventh house (partner). The eleventh house indicating the partners of one's children because it is the seventh (partners) from the fifth (children).

Earth Signs—The three signs of the zodiac in the Earth Element: Taurus, Virgo and Capricorn.

Eclipse—The passage of one celestial body in front, or into the shadow, of another as when the Moon goes into the shadow of the earth or the Sun is blocked by the Moon.

Ecliptic—The apparent path of the Sun around the Earth.

Ego—The center of consciousness.

Electional Astrology—The field of astrology that seeks the best time to hold or initiate an event. A chart is set up for the time in the future that would best suit the event.

Elements—The division of the signs of the zodiac into four fundamental natures: fire, earth, air and water.

Ephemeris—A table that charts the position of the planets, usually daily, at a set time (midnight or mid-day) and set place (Greenwich, England).

Erinyes—The Greek goddesses of vengeance, usually three, born from drops of blood falling from the severed genitals of Oranus.

Eros—1) The Greek god of love, also known as the Roman Cupid or Amor. 2) Asteroid 433 Eros orbiting between Mars and Venus. 3) The Greek word for love and creativity associated with passionate union and lasting transformation.

Fire Signs—The three signs of the zodiac in the fire element: Aries, Leo and Sagittarius.

Fixed Signs—Those signs of the zodiac associated with the succedent houses, Taurus, Leo, Scorpio and Aquarius and the four Greek types of love, Epithemia, Phillia, Eros and Agape.

Fixed Stars—The actual stars, as opposed to the "wandering stars" or planets.

Fortuna—The Arabic Part of Fortune derived by adding the Ascendant to the Moon and subtracting the Sun.

Gaia—The Greek earth goddess, sister/mate of Ouranus.

Geocentric—Astrology that places the earth in the center of the chart as opposed to heliocentric, which is solar centered.

Hades—The Greek god of the underworld, counterpart of the Roman Pluto.

Hekate—The Greek goddess of the Moon and the underworld.

Hephaistos—Greek god of the forge, the lame master craftsman and husband to Aphrodite.

Hermes—The Greek counterpart of the Roman Mercury, messenger of the gods.

Hera—The Greek goddess of marriage, sister/wife of Zeus and counterpart to the Roman Juno.

Horary—A field of astrology that sets up a chart for the moment in time a specific question is asked. The resultant chart is then interpreted in a systematic fashion to amplify the question by defining the people involved, problems associated with it, background and likely flow of events, thus an answer is given. The premise is that at the time a question is asked, the quality and meaning of that question is reflected in the specific moment it was 'born'.

Imum Coeli—180 degrees from the Midheaven, the Nadir or lowest point in the chart.

Individual—A distinct and integrated personality.

Individuation—The method of becoming an individual.

Intercepted—A sign that is completely contained within a house and does not appear on either cusp.

Juno—(1) The divine consort and sister of Jupiter, goddess of marriage and the well-being of women. Counterpart of the Greek Hera. (2) Asteroid 3 Juno orbiting between Mars and Jupiter.

Jupiter—The Roman counterpart of the Greek Zeus, king of the gods of Mt. Olympus.

Lechesis—One of the three Greek sisters of Fate, Lechesis measures the thread determining the length of mortal life.

Libido—Psychic energy including but not limited to sexual energy.

Luminaries—The Sun and Moon.

Mars The Roman god of war, similar to the Greek Ares but more civilized and focused.

Medium Coeli—The Midheaven or apex of the chart.

Mercury—The Roman counterpart of the Greek Hermes, messenger of the gods.

Midpoint—The ecliptic half way between two planets or points in a chart or between two separate charts.

Midheaven—The MC or Medium Coeli. The highest point a planet or point can reach in the chart.

Moira—The Greek goddess of fate, also known as Necessity or Ananke.

Mutable Signs—The four signs of the zodiac associated with the cadent houses: Gemini, Virgo, Sagittarius and Pisces.

Mutual Reception—When two planets are in each other's natural sign i.e. Moon in Aquarius and Uranus in Cancer.

Necessity—The Greek goddess of fate. Also known as Moira or Ananke.

Neptune—The Roman god of the mysterious sea, similar to the Greek Poseidon.

Nodes—The Lunar Nodes, Moon's Nodes or Dragon's Head and Tail, are points in the astrological chart where the Moon ascends (North Node) and descends (South Node) the ecliptic.

Orbs—The range of degrees between aspecting planets and points that is considered effective. Usually between one and thirteen degrees.

Ouranos—The original Greek sky god that produced the race of Titans.

Pallas Athene—(1) Greek goddess of wisdom, strategy, arts and crafts. Also known as Athene, counterpart to the Roman Minerva. (2) Asteroid 2 Pallas Athene, orbiting between Mars and Jupiter.

Parallel—Planets are parallel when they have the same declination, or number of degrees, north or south of the equator.

Persephone—The Greek daughter of Demeter, abducted by Hades/Pluto and made queen of the underworld.

Planets (astrological)—The major and minor planets of the solar system, including the Sun and Moon.

Pluto—The Roman god of the underworld, counterpart to the Greek Hades.

Pollux—The mortal Twin of Castor in the constellation of Gemini.

Poseidon—Brother of Zeus. He was the Greek god of the sea, weather and earth quakes, similar to the Roman Neptune.

Progressions—Any number of astrological systems that advances the position of the natal planets and relate them back as transits. Also called directions.

Projection—The act of attributing an inner goal, desire or quality onto another person place or thing. The individual who 're-ceives' the projection will illicit a strong emotional response from the one projecting, who usually remains unaware of the mechanism in play.

Prometheus—The Greek Titan that stole fire from the gods to give to humankind. He was punished by Zeus for his offering of light and consciousness.

Psyche—1) The sum of the conscious and the unconscious (soul). 2) The mortal beauty who fell in love with Eros. 3) Asteroid 16 Psyche.

Quadruplicities—The four zodiac signs that have the same modality or form of motion: cardinal, fixed or mutable.

Radical—Natal or nativity: all pertaining to the birth chart.

Radix—Same as radical. Referring to the birth chart.

Rhea—A Greek earth goddess, a Titan and sister/mate to Kronos (Saturn).

Repression—The expulsion from consciousness of an unsavory experience or archetype. This may be a conscious or unconscious eviction.

Retrograde—A planet which appears to be moving backward, westward, in the sky. This occurs when the planet is closest to the earth.

Returns—This occurs when a transiting planet or luminary has traveled a complete circuit around the zodiac and has returned to the exact degree it occupied in the birth chart. The Moon returns approximately every twenty-nine days, the Sun approximately every 365. A chart may be cast for the given moment of any planet's return.

Ruler (rulerships)—Each planet is said to rule over assigned zodiac signs i.e. The Moon rules Cancer. Houses are ruled by the ruler of the sign on the cusp, also called Lord of a house. The *chart ruler* is usually the ruler of the ascendant although some use the ruler of the Sun.

Saturn—The Roman counterpart to Kronos (also Kronus).

Self—The individual's archetype of wholeness.

Separating—A planet is separating when is moving away from an exact aspect with a slower moving planet or point in the chart.

Shadow—The unconscious side of the individual of which they are unaware. Although the shadowed traits may be creative as well as destructive, they are generally abhorred, rejected or ignored. The shadow appears in dreams as a same sex individual and may illicit intense fear and loathing. Acceptance and assimilation of shadowed material generally results in increased energy and libido.

Stationary—A stationary planet appears to be holding still, moving neither direct nor retrograde. This occurs just prior to an apparent change of direction.

Stellium—A group of four (sometimes considered five) or more planets in a given sign or house.

Succedent Houses—Those houses that follow the angular ones: second, fifth, eighth and eleventh.

Symbol—The expression of something essentially indefinable in rational, logical terms by use of right brain, non-linear means.

Synchronicity—The meaningful coincidence of an inner psychic event and an outer physical one that can not be explained by causality.

Transits—The movement of the planets and points as they relate back to a fixed point such as the natal chart.

Uranus—The Roman counterpart to the original sky god, Ouranos.

Unconscious—All that is unfathomable or currently unacknowledged in the psyche by consciousness.

Venus—The Roman counterpart of the Greek Aphrodite, goddess of love.

Vesta—(1) Goddess of the hearth, flame and torch, virgin/harlot possessed by no man. Vestal virgins tended the eternal flame in her temple. (2) Asteroid 4 Vesta, orbiting between Mars and Jupiter. The only asteroid bright enough to be seen by the naked eye.

Vocation—A calling, summoning. A career or pursuit for which one feels a particular calling (religious or otherwise) or a particular aptitude for. From the Latin *vocare,* to call.

Void of Course—The Moon or any planet that makes no applying aspect before it changes sign.

Water Signs—The three signs of the zodiac in the water element: Cancer, Scorpio and Pisces.

Zodiac (tropical)—The belt of constellations around the ecliptic comprising the twelve astrological signs, divided into thirty degrees each, through which the planets appear to move.

Zeus—The Greek king of the gods, counterpart to the Roman Jupiter.

Suggested Reading List and Web Sites

AdZe, MiXXe's Angle on Aspects *Pursue all angles,* http://www.adze.com/astro/aspects.html

Alciato, Andrea *Book of Emblems* Ed. William Barker, Mark Fletham, Jean Guthrie Department of English Memorial University of Newfoundland. Emblem 110 Anteros, Which is the Love of Virtue, http://www.mun.ca/alciato/

American Federation of Astrologers: The official site of the national organization: http://www.astrologers.com/

Arroyo, Stephen *Astrology Karma and Transformation: The Inner Dimensions of the Birth Chart,* CRCS Publications Reno, Nevada 1978

Arroyo, Stephen *Relationships and Life Cycles: Modern Dimensions of Astrology,* CRCS Publications Reno, Nevada 1979

Asteroid 433 Eros: The Astrology of Love, http://www.nrg.com.au/~d-falcon/Eros.htm

Astrodienst, Astro*Intelligence and asteroid ephemeris on line.

HTTP://www.astro.com

Astro: Jon Dunn's site with articles on several advanced subjects, including asteroids and an asteroid ephemeris. http://jonathanclarkdunn.com/astro/index.shtml

The Astrology Matrix, online interactive astrology reports (real-time astrology/oracles), Astro*Index (online encyclopedia), online astrology bibliography, real-time search for charts from 20,000 celebrity charts, and more http://www.astrologysoftware.com

Astrology with Anthony Peña: A wealth of information and an excellent guide to over 700 sites http://www.astrology.about.com/

Begg, Ean *Myth and Today's Consciousness* Coventure Ltd. London SWl 1984

Bills, Rex E. *The Rulership Book,* American Federation of Astrologers, Tempe, Arizona

Bolen, Jean Shinoda *Goddesses in Every Woman: A New Psychology of Women,* Harper Colophon Books Harper & Row Publishers Inc. New York, NT 1984

Capra, F. *The Tao of Physics,* Bantam Books: New York 1983

Campbell, Joseph *Creative Mythology: The Masks of God*, Midlesex, England, Penguin Books, 1972

Campbell, Joseph *Occidental Mythology: The Masks of God,* Penguin Books Harmondsworth, Middlesex, England reprinted 1985

Carotenunto, Aldo *The Vertical Labyrinth*, Inner City Books, Toronto, Canada 1985

Chetwynd, Tom *A Dictionary of Symbols*, Paladin Grafton Books, a division of the Collins Publishing Group, London 1982

Chetwynd, Tom *Dictionary for Dreamers,* Paladin Grafton Books, a division of the Collins Publishing Group, London 1974

Chiron and Friends: Insightful information on astrology, particularly Chiron, The Centaurs and many asteroids http://www.geocities.com/SoHo/7969/ chiron_a.htm

CPA Press (Centre for Psychological Astrology London). Order transcripts and books from the Centre http://www.astrologer.com/cpa/cpapress.html

Elwell, Dennis *Cosmic Loom: The New Science of Astrology,* Unwin Hyman Limited London, England 1987

George, Demetra w/ Douglas Bloch, *Asteroid Goddesses: The Mythology, Psychology and Astrology of the Reemerging Feminine,* ACS Publications San Diego, CA 1986

Greene, Liz *Relating: An Astrological Guide to Living with Others on a Small Planet*, Samuel Weiser Inc. York Beach, Maine 1978

Greene, Liz *Barriers and Boundaries,* vol. 1, CPA Centre for Psychological Astrology Press, London 1998

Greene, Liz *The Astrology of Fate*, Samuel Weiser, Inc. York Beach, Maine, 1984

Greene, Liz *The Astrological Neptune and the Quest for Redemption*, Samuel Weiser Inc. York Beach, Maine 1996

Greene, Liz *The Outer Planets and Their Cycles: The Astrology of the Collective,* CRCS Publications, Reno Nevada USA 1983

Greene, Liz *Saturn: A New Look at an Old Devil*, Samuel Weiser, Inc. York Beach, Maine 1976

Greene & Arroyo *The Jupiter/Saturn Conference Lectures*, CRCS Publications, Reno, California 1984

Greene & Sasportas, *The Development of the Personality: Seminars in Psychological Astrology, Vol 1, 2,3 & 4* Samuel Weiser, Inc. York Beach, Maine 1987

Hand, Robert *Horoscope Symbols*, Para Research Inc, Inc. Gloucester, Ma USA 1981

Hand, Robert *Planets in Composite, Analyzing Human Relationships*, Para Research Inc., Whistlestop Mall, Rockport, Massachusetts 01966 1975

Hickey, Isabel *Astrology: A Cosmic Science,* Altiere Press Bridgeport, Connecticut 1975

Hone, Margaret *The modern Text Book of Astrology*, L.N. Fowler & Co. Ltd. Romford, Essex 1951

Idemon, Richard *Breaking the Silver Cord,* 2 tapes #RI-203 Pegasus Tapes: Audio Cassettes on Astrological, Psychological and Mythological Themes. P.O. Box 419 , Santa Ysabel, CA

Idemon, Richard *The Magic Thread: Astrological chart Interpretation Using Depth Psychology,* Samuel Weiser Inc., York Beach, Maine 1996

Idemon, Richard *Through The Looking Glass: A Search for the Self in the Mirror of Relationships*, Samuel Weiser Inc, York

Beach, Maine 1992

Jacobson, Ivy M. Goldstein *Simplified Horary Astrology,* Pasadena Lithographers Pasadena, California 1960

Leo, Alan *The Progressed Horoscope* L.N. Fowler & Co. Ltd London 1969

Levine, Peter A. *Waking the Tiger: Healing Trauma,* North Atlantic Books, Berkeley, CA 1997

McFadden, Lucy A. Christopher T. Russell, Andrew F. Cheng *The Near Earth Asteroid Mission to 433 Eros,* Originally appeared in EOS, Trans AGU, 77, 73 and 79, 1996 http://www-ssc.igpp.ucla.edu/NEAR/over.html

Marin, Peter *The Fury of Eros,* Harper's Magazine02/94 v288:n1725.

Moore, Thomas, *The Planets Within: The Astrological Psychology of Marsilio Ficino,* Lindisfarne Press, Great Barrington, MA 1990

New Larousse Encyclopedia of Mythology, Felix Guirand (editor) Hamlyn Publishing Group Limited, Middlesex, England 1959

Ovid's Metamorphoses, Book I, Daphne, Crane, Gregory R. (ed.) The Perseus Project, http://www.perseus.tufts.edu

Parabola*, The Magazine of Myth and Tradition,* New York, NY http://www.parabola.org/

Parada, Carlos *Greek Mythology Link* Hosted by HSA, Brown University http://hsa.brown.edu/~maicar/http://www.perseus.tufts.edu

Roberts, Richard *From Eden to Eros: Origins of the Put Down of Women,* Vernal Equinox Press, San Anselmo, CA 1985

Sargent, Lois Haines *How to Handle Your Human Relationships* American Federation of Astrologers, Inc. Tempe, Arizona 1970

Sasportas, Howard *Direction and Destiny in the Birth Chart*, vol 10, CPA Centre for Psychological Astrology Press, London 1998

Sasportas, Howard *The Gods of Change,* Arkana (Penguin Books) London, England 1989

Sasportas, Howard *The Twelve Houses: An Astrological Guide to Life's Possibilities,* The Aquarian Press Wellingborough, Northhamptonshire England 1985 Copy right now: HarperCollins Ltd. Harmmersmith, London

Wickenburg, Joanne, Director of SEARCH, P.O. Box 162

Nortgate Station, Seattle, WA 98125 USA

Wickenburg, Joanne, *Intercepted Signs: Environment VS Destiny,* Search, Seattle, WA 1978

Vocational Rulerships

Advertising—Mercury, Mars, Jupiter, Gemini, Sagittarius

Aerospace, Astronomy, Aviation—Jupiter, Uranus, Aries, Sagittarius, Aquarius, ninth

Agriculture, Farming—Saturn, Ceres, Capricorn, Fourth, Tenth

Alchemists—Pluto, Mercury, Gemini, Scorpio

Alcoholics Anonymous/Addiction Counselor—Neptune, Aquarius, Pisces, eleventh, twelfth

Alternative Health, Herbs, Homeopathy, Aroma Therapy—Mercury, Pluto, Chiron, Ceres, Neptune, Virgo, Pisces, Scorpio, sixth, twelfth

Animation—Traditional: Mercury, Neptune, Venus, fifth; computer: Mercury, Uranus, fifth, sixth

Archeology—Mars, Saturn, Pluto, Scorpio, Sagittarius, Capricorn

Architecture—Mercury, Venus, Saturn, Uranus, Taurus, Virgo, Capricorn, tenth

Armed Forces—Mars, Aries, Virgo, Sagittarius

Arts & Entertainment (film, drama, music, visual & performing arts)—Sun, Venus, Neptune, Leo, Libra, Pisces, third, fifth, seventh, ninth, twelfth

Astrologer—Mercury, Uranus, Aquarius, Regulus

Athletes, Sports, Fitness, Acrobats, Gymnasts—Sun, Mars, Jupiter, Aries, Sagittarius, Pallas

Baker—Moon, Cancer

Beauty Therapies, Fashion, Make-up Artistry—Venus, Uranus, Neptune, Taurus, Libra, Sagittarius

Blacksmith—Mars, Jupiter, Virgo, Pisces

Body Workers, Massage, Physiotherapy—Venus, Mars, Saturn, Chiron, Pluto, Taurus, Aries, Virgo, Capricorn, sixth

Breast-feeding Counselors—Moon, Venus, Uranus, Cancer, Libra, Aquarius, seventh, eleventh

Business Partnerships—Venus, Pluto, Libra, Scorpio, seventh, eighth

Butcher—Mars, Pluto, Scorpio, eighth

Child Care—Moon, Mercury, Saturn, Cancer, Aquarius, fourth, tenth, eleventh

Chiropractic—Saturn, Chiron, Capricorn

Civil or Social Services—Sun, Moon, Venus, Uranus, Cancer, Libra, Sagittarius, Aquarius, eleventh, twelfth

Cleaners, Janitors, Porters—Mercury, Gemini, Virgo, sixth

Construction Industry—Mars, Jupiter, Saturn, Aries, Capricorn, fourth, sixth, tenth

Counselors and Therapists—Venus, Pluto, Chiron, Jupiter, Mercury, seventh, ninth

Couriers, Cab Drivers, Delivery—Mercury, Jupiter, Gemini, third

Critics—Sun, Mercury, Saturn, Virgo, Capricorn, sixth, tenth

Dancers—Venus, Libra

Dentistry—Sun, Mercury, Saturn, Uranus, Pluto, Virgo, Scorpio, sixth

Diplomacy—Mercury, Venus, Neptune, Pluto, Libra, Sagittarius, seventh, ninth, eleventh

Electricians—Uranus, Aquarius, sixth

Engineers—Chemical: Moon, Neptune, Pisces; civil: Saturn; electrical, Sun, Mars, Jupiter, Uranus, Leo, Scorpio, Aquarius; mechanical: Mercury, Mars; metallurgical: Uranus; mining: Saturn; sound: Mercury, Uranus, Neptune, Aquarius, Pisces

Equestrian—Jupiter, Saturn, Chiron, Mars, Virgo, Sagittarius, Pisces, sixth, twelfth

Finances, Banking, Accounting—Sun, Venus, Saturn, Taurus, Leo, Virgo, Capricorn, second, fifth, eighth

Fine Crafts (jewelry, locksmith, carving, sewing)—Mercury, Venus, Mars, Gemini, Virgo, sixth

Fishing Industry—Moon, Neptune, Pisces

Florists—Venus

Food, Beverages, Restaurants, Cafes—Moon, Mercury, Venus, Ceres, Gemini, Cancer, Virgo, sixth; alcoholic beverages: Neptune, Pisces; foreign cuisine: Jupiter, Sagittarius, ninth

Grocer—Moon, Mercury, Taurus, Cancer, Virgo

Hospitality Industry—Sun, Moon, Mercury, Venus, Jupiter,

Gemini, Cancer, Leo, Sagittarius, Aquarius, third, fifth, sixth, eleventh

Industrial Worker, Assembly Line—Mercury, Virgo, sixth

Informer, Undercover Agent—Neptune, Pluto, Scorpio, Pisces, twelfth

Informant (tourist guide, gather/disseminating information)—Mercury, Jupiter, Gemini, Virgo, Sagittarius, third, sixth

Inspector—Mercury, Virgo

Institutions—Hospitals: Neptune, Pluto, Pisces, twelfth; prisons: Neptune, Pluto, Scorpio, Pisces, twelfth; university: Mercury, Jupiter, Sagittarius, ninth; lending institutions: Sun, Moon, Mercury, Pluto, Taurus, Leo, Scorpio, second, eighth; charities: Sun, Neptune, Leo, Pisces, twelfth; relief work, Peace Corps: Moon, Neptune, Pluto. Cancer, Scorpio, Pisces, sixth, twelfth

Interior Designer—Venus, Libra

Labor (manual, skilled, voluntary, hard work)—Saturn, Virgo, Capric9orn, sixth,. twelfth

Legal, Law Enforcement, Justice—Mercury, Venus, Mars, Jupiter, Pluto, Libra, Scorpio, Sagittarius, eighth, ninth, twelfth

Linguist—Mercury, Jupiter, Gemini, Virgo, Sagittarius, third, sixth, ninth

Literary Pursuits, Editing, Publishing, Writing, Bookstores—Moon, Mercury, Jupiter, Neptune, Cancer, Gemini, Virgo, Sagittarius, third, sixth, ninth

Management—Moon, Jupiter, Saturn, Uranus, Cancer, Libra, Sagittarius, Capricorn, Aquarius, tenth

Marine Biology, Oceanography—Moon, Mercury, Neptune, Gemini, Cancer, Pisces, third, twelfth

Martial Arts—Mars, Chiron, Pallas, Aries, Libra, Sagittarius, first, sixth

Mechanics (auto)—Mars, Uranus, third

Medicine, Doctor, Surgeon, Health Care Professional—Mercury, Mars, Saturn, Chiron, Neptune, Pluto, Virgo, Scorpio, Pisces, sixth, eighth, twelfth

Midwifery—Sun, Moon, Mercury, Pluto, Ceres, Juno, Gemini, Leo, Sagittarius, Scorpio, fifth, seventh, eighth

Natural Sciences, Biochemistry, Geology, Meteorology—Sun, Moon, Saturn, Uranus, Cancer, Taurus, Capricorn,

Aquarius

New Age Speaker, Group Leader, Proponent—Jupiter, Uranus, Sagittarius, Aquarius, eleventh

Nutritionist—Moon, Mercury, Cancer, Virgo, sixth

Organizations, Associations, Groups, Unions and Clubs—Venus, Uranus, Aquarius, eleventh

Paleontology—Saturn, Uranus, Sagittarius, Capricorn

Pathologist, Mortician, Undertaker, Funeral Services—Saturn, Pluto, Scorpio, Capricorn, Pisces, eighth

Photography—Venus, Neptune, Libra, Pisces, fifth

Physicist—Uranus, Neptune, Pluto, Sagittarius, Aquarius, Pisces

Psychiatry, Mental Health Technician—Moon, Neptune, Pluto, twelfth

Politicians—Sun, Pluto, Leo, Scorpio, Sagittarius

Quarry Worker (large machinery)—Mars, Jupiter, Saturn, Capricorn

Quarantine and Customs—Jupiter, Saturn, Pluto, Capricorn, ninth

Radio & Television, Radar, World Wide Web—Mercury, Uranus, Jupiter, Aquarius, Sagittarius, third, ninth, eleventh

Radiology—Uranus, Pluto, Virgo, Scorpio, Aquarius, sixth, eighth, twelfth

Real Estate, Sales, Investment, Speculation—Sun, Moon, Mercury, Jupiter, Cancer, Leo, Libra, Sagittarius, fourth, seventh, eighth

Religious Studies, Vocations—Jupiter, Neptune, Sagittarius, ninth, twelfth

Rescue Team, Ambulance, Emergence Medicine, Disaster Squad, Lifeguard—Mars, Uranus, Neptune, Pluto, Aries, Scorpio, Sagittarius, Pisces, seventh, eighth, eleventh, twelfth

Research—Mercury, Jupiter, Uranus, Pluto, Gemini, Scorpio, Sagittarius, Aquarius, third, eighth, ninth, twelfth

Sales, Marketing, PR, Advertising—Sun, Mercury, Mars, Jupiter, Aries, Gemini, Sagittarius, third, sixth, ninth, tenth

Sanitation Technician—Saturn, Pluto, Scorpio, eighth

Scientist, Mathematician—Mercury, Uranus, Pluto, Gemini, Virgo, Scorpio, Sagittarius, Aquarius

Secretary, Clerical, Bookkeeping—Mercury, Venus, Saturn, Gemini, Virgo, Libra, Capricorn, third, sixth, seventh, tenth, eleventh

Sex Trade, Sex Worker—Mercury, Venus, Mars, Pluto, Taurus, Virgo, Scorpio

Tax Agent—Mercury, Mars, Pluto, Scorpio, eighth

Teaching & Training, Education—Mercury, Jupiter, Saturn, Chiron, Uranus, Pluto, Gemini, Sagittarius, third, ninth

Technology (information and telecommunications)—Mercury, Uranus, Gemini, Sagittarius, Aquarius, third, sixth, eleventh

Transport Industry—Ground (train, bus, car): Mercury, Mars, Gemini, Sagittarius; air: Jupiter, Uranus, Sagittarius, Aquarius

Travel and Tourist Industry—Mercury, Venus, Jupiter, Sagittarius, ninth

Veterinary Medicine—Mercury, Mars, Jupiter, Uranus, Neptune, Virgo, Scorpio, third, sixth, eighth

Wicca, Magic—Saturn, Neptune, Pluto, Chiron, Vesta, Virgo, Pisces, sixth

Wine Maker, Merchant, Vineyards—Venus, Jupiter, Neptune, Taurus, Sagittarius, Pisces

Zoologist—Jupiter, Saturn, Pluto, Virgo, Sagittarius, Pisces

End Notes

1. Elwell, Dennis, *The Cosmic Loom: The New Science of Astrology*, Unwin Hyman, London 1987, p. 166.

2. ibid, pp. 168-170.

3. Tolkein, JRR, *The Lord of the Rings*, Houghton Mifflin Company, Boston MA 1974.

4. P. Ovidius Naso, *Metamorphoses* (ed. Brookes More): book 10, line 143 [Book 10].

5. *The Fugitive*, directed by Andrew Davis, co-written by Ray Huggins (characters), Warner Brothers USA 1993.

6. *A Couch in New York*, directed and written by Chantal Alterman, Polygram Film Entertainment USA 1996.

7. *Independence Day*, directed and written by Roland Emmerich, 20th Century Fox USA 1996.

8. *Goldfinger*, based on a novel by Ian Fleming, directed by Guy Hamilton, United Artists Films USA 1964.

9. *Alice*, directed and written by Woody Allen, Orion Pictures USA 1990.

10. *The Devil's Advocate*, directed by Taylor Hackford, novel by Andrew Neiderman, Warner Bros. USA 1997.

11. Wolf, directed by Mile Nichols, written by Jim Harrison, Columbia Pictures USA 1994.

12. Raiders of the Lost Ark, directed by Steven Spielberg, written by George Lucas, Paramount Pictures USA 1981.

13. *Lawrence of Arabia*, directed by David Lean, based on the autobiography *The 7 Pillars of Wisdom* by T.E. Lawrence, Columbia Pictures 1962

14. *Erin Brocovich*, directed by Steven Soderbergh, written by Susannah Grant, Jersey Films Production 2000

15. *The Fisher King*, directed by Terry Gilliam, written by Richard LaGravenese, Columbia Pictures 1991.

16. The angles are the natural cross in the chart—Ascendant-Descendant, Midheaven-Immun Coeli.

17. If no planets are in the first house or near the Ascendant, note the first planet to rise, no matter how far away.

18. Amoral: free of moral judgments. Neither moral nor immoral.

19. Sasportas, Howard, *The Twelve Houses*, The Aquarian Press, Wellingborough, Northamptonshire 1985, p. 66.

20. Hickey, Isabel, *Astrology: A Cosmic Science*, Altieri Press, Bridgeport, Connecticut 1975, p. 181.

21. Hickey, p. 62.

22. Sasportas, Howard, *The Luminaries: Seminars in Psychological Astrology*, Vol. 3, Samuel Weiser, York Beach, Maine 1992, p. 124.

23. Greene, Liz, *Relating: An Astrological Guide to Living with Others on a Small Planet*, Samuel Weiser, York Beach, Maine, p. 33.

24. Hesiod, Theogony: line 90 [Theogony] Crane, Gregory R., The Perseus Project, www.perseus.tufts. edu, January 2001.

25. Moore, Thomas, *The Planets Within: The Astrological Psychology of Marsilio Ficino*, Lindisfarne Press, Great Barrington, Massachusetts, p. 159.

26. See: Ean Begg, *Myth and Today's Consciousness*, Coventure, London, 1984.

190

27. Ibid., p. 20.

28. Alciato, Andrea, *Book of Emblems*, William Barker, Mark Fletham, Jean Guthrie, Department of English, Memorial University of Newfoundland, Emblem 8 www.mun.ca/alciato/, January 2001.

29. Moore, Thomas, *The Planets Within: The Astrological Psychology of Marsilio Ficino*, Lindisfarne Press, Great Barrington, Massachusetts 1990, p. 143.

30. Jung, Carl Gustave, *Memories, Dreams, Reflections*, Ed Aniela Jaffe, trans. by Richard and Clara Winston, Vintage Books, A Division of Random House, New York 1965, p. 208.

31. Hickey, Isabel, *Astrology: A Cosmic Science*, Altieri Press, Bridgeport, Connecticut 1975.

32. Ibid., p. 198.

33. Ivy M. Goldstein Jacobson, *Simplified Horary Astrology*, Pasadena Lithographers, Pasadena, California 1960, p. 52.

34. Hone, Margaret, *The Modern Text Book of Astrology*, L.N. Fowler & Co., Ltd., Romfort, Essex 1951, p. 280.

35. Falconer, Kim, *Asteroid 433 Eros: The Astrology of Love*, www.nrg.com.au/~d-falcon/Eros.htm, February 2001.

36. Hedy Lamarr, *Los Angeles Times*, August 30, 1997, www.rocamora.org/Page85.html, December 2000.

37. Anthony Loder, Hedy Lamarr's son and president of U.S. Phones, site by Courtney Baalman, www.hoxie.org/news99/senior99/hedy1.html, January 2001.

38. Birth data source: Matrix Win*Star 2.01, Matrix Software, Big Rapids, Michigan.

39. For a detailed investigation into Hemingway's emotional life, see Idemon, Richard, *The Magic Threat: Astrological Chart Interpretation Using Depth Psychology*, Samuel Weiser, York Beach, Maine 1996, pp. 231-242.

40. George Plimpton interview 1958(?), In Plimpton, ed., Writers at Work: Second Series, 1963.

41. Elwell, Dennis, *The Cosmic Loom: The New Science of Astrology*, Unwin Hyman, London 1987, p. 188.

42. Birth data source: Matrix Win*Star 2.01, Matrix Software, Big Rapids, Michigan.

Index

30 Urania, 140
4 Vesta, 143
Astrologer, 23, 92, 95, 101, 137, 140, 148 ,181, 185
Astrology, 81, 156, 132, 140
Athene, 174
Atropos, 175
audacity, 100
author, 167

B

banking, 34
biology, 100
black virgin, 92
body work, 76 See Massage
Brice, Fannie, 102
Browning, Elizabeth Barrette, 143
Business partnerships See Partnerships

C

Cadent Houses, 30 , 175
Cancer, 2, 8, 9, 10, 11, 42, 92, 170
Capricorn, 2, 20, 21, 22, 23, 99
Cardinal Signs, 2, 9, 14, 20, 22, 172
Castor, 175
Cerberus, 140
Ceres, 175
chart ruler, 30
Child Care, 134, 186
children, 54, 100, 115, 155, 166, 168, 176
Chiron, 32, 36, 40, 41, 45, 46, 50, 55, 56, 61, 62, 66, 71, 76, 81, 86, 100, 133, 175
Chiropractics, 36, 186
Churchill, Winston, 141
Clerical, 189
Clotho, 175
Collective Conscious, 26, 175
commerce, 34
commitment, 136
communication, 37, 151

conjunction, 92, 121, 128, 139, 140, 148
Consciousness, 175
Construction, 186
counseling, 75
Counselors, 185, See also Therapists
Cousteau, Jacques, 143
coworkers, 57
Crafts, 186
creative arts, 69
Critics, 186
crossroads, 93
Crowd surfing, 108
crystals, 100
cusps, 29, 30, 42

D

daimon, 147, 176
dance,, 6, 21, 26, 47, 49, 50, 54, 77
Dancers, 186
dark feminine, 137
Deities
Aphrodite, 144, 157
Apollo, 90, 150
Ares, 152
Artemis, 90
Athene, 135
Circe, 140
Demeter, 154, 158
Dionysus, 176
Ereshkagal, 92
Eros, 144
Gaea, 155, 157
Hades, 140, 154
Hecate, 92
Hecatonchires, 157
Helios, 134
Hephaestus, 141
Hera, 135, 154
Hermes, 151
Hestia, 154

86, 104, 158, 166

V

Venus, 5, 14, 31, 32, 33, 34, 35, 39, 44, 49, 54, 60, 65, 69, 74, 75, 79, 80, 84, 94, 152, 154, 181
vertere, 119
Vertex, 119, 122, 134
Vertumnus, 121
Vesta, 181
Veterinary Medicine, 189
victim, 27, 101
Virgo, 2, 12, 13, 14, 15, 27, 73, 90, 169
Vocation, 181

W

WATER, 2, 9, 16, 17, 25, 26, 34, 35, 37, 85
Water Signs, 181
Water-bearer, 23

Webster, Noah, 103
welfare, 56
Wickenburg, Joanne, 185
windfalls, 66
Wine Maker, 189
Witchcraft, 53, 134, 189
wounded healer, 156
wounding, 100
Wright, Wilber, 142
writers, 71
writing, 38, 40, 167

Y

Yeats, W.B., 138
yoga, 36, 39, 40, 49, 54, 66

Z

Zero Degree Aries Point, 115
Zeus, 181 See also Deities
zodiac, 1, 3, 7, 12, 20,181
zombies, 158
Zoologist, 189